D1506410

THE LITTLE PREACHER

ELIZABETH PRENTISS

THE LITTLE PREACHER

ELIZABETH PRENTISS

HSM PUBLISHING

92-594 Palailai St., Kapolei, HI 96707
www.HSMpublishing.com / 1-888-330-4718

HSM Publishing
92-594 Palailai Street
Kapolei, HI 96707
1-888-330-4718 / www.HSMpublishing.com
ISBN 1-879737-10-8

©2002 HSM Publishing
All rights reserved under International and Pan-American Copyright
Conventions. No part of this book may be reproduced in any form or
by any electronic or mechanical means including informational
storage and retrieval systems without the expressed permission from
the publisher in writing.

Direct all inquires to -
HSM Publishing 92-594 Palailai St., Kapolei, HI 96707

Book and Cover Design: Anthony Rotolo

Prentiss, Elizabeth (1818 - 1878)
    The Little Preacher
Suggested Subject Headings:
1. Christian Fiction - Family
I. Title

Manufactured in the United States of America

Preface

Elizabeth Prentiss (1818-1878) was a woman who loved her Savior. She is best known for two writings , a hymn and a very beautiful story. The hymn, More Love to Thee, O Christ, can be found in most church hymnals today. The beautiful story is Stepping Heavenward, a classic in Christian women's literature.

The Little Preacher, written in 1867, is a tale for all ages. Set in the Black Forest of Germany, Mrs. Prentiss spins a realistic tale of a family striving for survival, but lacking true knowledge of their Savior. Within the pages of this little book you will find a hard-hearted father, an extraordinary boy, a mother and grandmother praying continually for them all. It is a story of the life changing power of Jesus Christ and of prayers that avail much.

Elisabeth Elliot has called it, "A lovely book...the character of the grandmother is beautifully realized, and the love of God pervades the story."

It is to you dear reader that we give this tale. May it thrill your soul and move you closer to your Creator.

AnnMarie Friedrick
Kathleen Pethtel
HSM Publishing

THE LITTLE PREACHER

ELIZABETH PRENTISS

1

In a little village of the Black Forest there sat, one Sunday afternoon, on a bench before a cottage door, two persons engaged in conversation, a man and a woman. Both were tall and well made, both ruddy and fair, and the striking likeness they bore each other made it seem probable that they were sister and brother. In reality they were mother and son.

"I am getting on in the world vastly well without your blessed father," she was saying. "People tell me I have no sooner touched a bit of land than it begins to bear gold."

"I hope I have inherited that talent," he returned,

laughing, "for to tell the truth, mother, I came up today to invite you to my wedding."

"Your wedding! And when did I ever give you permission to take a wife, Max Steiner?"

Max moved uneasily in his seat.

"You seem to forget that I am no longer a boy," he said.

"There is no danger," she retorted, "while you act like one."

Max rose to his feet.

"Goodbye, mother," he said.

"Sit down, you foolish child. And when is this famous wedding to come off?"

"Next week. Doris said—"

"Doris! What Doris?"

"Ah! mother, you know; the old schoolteacher's daughter, Doris."

"And what does she bring you?"

"Not much besides herself and her mother."

"Her mother! That shall never be!"

"There's no use arguing about it," said Max, "I can't have one without the other."

"Then I forbid the marriage."

"Mother," said Max, "I am a fullgrown man. I am able to manage my own affairs, and mean to do it. It is true we shall have to begin in a small way, and if I could help it I would not have the expense or bother of a mother-in-law in the house, but I can't help it."

"Now, there is the miller's daughter Lore who

will have a dowry worth looking after; take her Max, and I'll say no more against your marrying. A mother-in-law in the house is like a crackling thorn, meddling and ordering will be her only business. And you are one to be master in your own house."

"I rather think I am," said Max, setting his teeth together, "and that is one reason why I have fixed my eyes upon Doris. She is as quiet as a little mouse, and will oppose me in nothing."

"I hate your little mice!" she cried.

"Well, mother, there's just where we differ. I like them. The girls that go to the rough dances and let the fellows toss them about may be very well for an evening's frolic, but when it comes to settling down for life, a man wants a wife that hasn't been made so free with."

"As to that, you know very well that Doris' mother has never let her say her soul was her own. She has kept her always pinned to her side, singing hymns and saying prayers, otherwise she would have gone flaunting and giggling about like all the other girls."

"At any rate, you can't deny that she is the prettiest girl in the village," said Max.

"Humph!"

"And once a man gets to loving a girl, well—"

"So he loves her, does he? To think of that, now! Ha! ha! And perhaps he is in love with the girl's mother also!"

"Well, then, if it comes to that, I do love her!" cried Max, rising angrily from his seat. "I don't pretend to say prayers or to sing hymns myself, but I would like a wife none the less for doing both, if she took care not do it in a self-righteous way. And, at all events, the thing is settled. I shall marry Doris, and nobody else!"

He seized his cap, and with rapid strides proceeded homeward down the mountain path that led to his own village.

"Thank heaven, one does not have to marry one's mother!" he said to himself. "I shall get on better with Doris. Two redhaired people in one house is too much. I am thankful she is not quick-tempered as my mother is, and as I am."

Doris was the daughter of the schoolteacher, and had been brought up in great poverty and to much hard work. Her father had taught her all he knew himself, which, to be sure, was not much, and had been dead some years. Her mother had been trained in the hard school of sorrow. All she had left to the human eye was this one child, out of a home once full of sons and daughters. But, in reality, she possessed a character disciplined and tempered to the last degree of sweetness and cheerfulness. She was rich in faith, rich in love to God and man, rich in foretastes of a life to come, in which there would never be felt the sting of poverty, and where even the shadow of death could never fall.

"Dear mother," said Doris, "I am asking a great deal of you when I ask you to leave our native village, and go with me to a new home."

"Nay, my Doris, but it is I who ask a great deal in going there. It is true, I do not gladly leave our dear Herr Pastor, who has taught me so much. And our good neighbors we shall miss likewise! But that will pass, and I shall try to make Max's home a happy one."

"There's no doubt of that!" said Doris, smiling, "but I know you always hoped to die where you have lived so long, and I know it is going to be hard for you to make this change. But Max says he cannot and will not live here, so near to his mother. She vexes and frets him so. Ah! I am glad you are not like her, dear mother!"

The marriage took place, and Max established his wife as comfortably as he could in the house adjoining the little shed where he carried on his business, for he was a carpenter. The lessons of economy, instilled into him by his mother, bore their fruit in his new home, where even the necessities of life were dealt out with a careful hand.

Doris entered with docility into all his wishes. She ordered her household discreetly, wasted nothing, and knew no idle moment. Her mother helped her in all the tasks suited to her strength. She was no crackling thorn, but left Max full liberty to be master in his own house. Though she was never jolly, as Doris was in moments of exuberant health and happiness, she was so uniformly cheerful that the very sunshine itself hardly did so much to give light within the house. This was no matter of accident, yet she could not herself have told the philosophy of her calm content. Hers had been a life full of disappointment and bereavement. Her heart was one full of sensibility and passion. Why should it not lie torn and bleeding in the dust? Let those answer who, after years of suffering and prayers and tears, have learned:

> *To nurse the cage'd sorrow*
> *Till the captive sings!*

As for Max, he was upright and industrious. He wasted neither time nor money at the alehouse, and worked early and late, in doors and out.

Twice every Sunday they all put on their holiday clothes, locked the house door, and went to church. When at night Max put off these garments, he put off, with them, all thought of religion, and gave himself up to toil and worldly care, and making and saving. Doris never admitted, even to herself, that he had his faults; that he was too proud to be affectionate and demonstrative, and that the hard race to make money was sharpening and hardening a temper not naturally good. She took care not to run against his peculiarities—as far, at least, as she knew how. And, above all, she loved him with the true-hearted loyalty of a faithful woman. Let anyone dare to say a word against her Max, and this "quiet mouse" of his had fire and passion enough in reserve to consume the offender.

In less than a year after their marriage she had spun linen enough to make the purchase of a cow. Accordingly, Max went to market in a neighboring village to choose one for her.

Here he met his mother, stalking about as with seven leagued boots, buying and selling.

"And what are you doing here?" she cried.

"My Doris has sent me to buy a cow," he returned; "the money she has earned herself."

"So you are already her errand boy! And how is the dear mother-in-law?"

"She is never very strong, but we get on wonderfully together."

"That sounds very well. But with one's mother one may safely speak out and out. Now let's have the truth, Max. She meddles and makes trouble, does she? Ah! but did not I warn you beforehand?"

"Mother, why will you try to exasperate me every time we meet? There is nothing to be said against Doris' mother."

"And the miller's daughter Lore has married the baker's son Franz, and has gone to live near you, they say. Think, whenever you see her, what you have lost."

Max turned away, full of disgust, and bought the cow with a ruffled spirit. The poor creature could not imagine what she had done that she should be driven to her new home with so many needless blows.

Doris came out to admire the purchase, and did not trouble herself with the thought that all the creature ate was to be sought for and carried to her by her own hands. She cut grass by the wayside, and brought home bundles of clover on her head. The cow cost them nothing but this labor, and her milk was a great comfort to them. The neighbors whispered among themselves that Doris gave away milk that had not been skimmed, now and then, and wondered if Max knew of this extravagance. If Max did not know it, it was because her right hand never knew what was done by the left when a case of real distress appeared.

Thus things went on till one day there came a new joy and a new care into the house.

"He's a beautiful boy, dear Max," said Doris, looking fondly down upon her firstborn son. "He is such a funny little likeness of you that I can't help laughing every time I look at him!"

"He has the red hair of the Steiners, and will have their hot blood," said Max.

"Red!" cried Doris, "Now, Max!"

"There's a tinge of red in it, I am sure," persisted Max. "And a fiery young colt you will have in him."

"Don't you like him, then?" asked Doris.

"The child is well enough," replied Max.

"If I dare say you will laugh at me, Max, but I must tell you what a strange dream I had last night. I thought we were in the church, and that it was beautifully lighted up, and everybody had on a new holiday suit. You had silver buttons on your scarlet vest, and the silver buckles at the knees, and looked as you did on our wedding day. And when the Herr Pastor rose in the pulpit, who should he be but our son, our little Herman here, grown to be a man, and actually become a clergyman!"

"A very silly dream," returned Max. "I don't look much like silver buckles, nor does that little lump of dough look much like a parson."

Having now said and done all that the occasion seemed to require, Max resumed his pipe, and cut short the interview with his first-born. Doris soon heard, through the open window, the sound of chopping and sawing.

"Ah!" she said joyfully to herself, "dear Max is making the bench under the linden tree that he has promised so long. Yes, my Herman, a nice seat for us in summer evenings, when you and your sisters and brothers will be playing about us. For brothers and sisters you must have, my little man, otherwise you will pine for lack of playfellows."

Meanwhile, Max worked steadily at the bench,

and he, too, had visions of children to come. But they were not "playing about." They were collecting fuel, and cutting grass and clover. They were gathering berries and hunting eggs. They were taking care of the cattle and feeding the hens. They were making amends, by every shift and turn, for all the money and all the trouble they cost.

Little Herman grew up to boyhood, and the other children followed at intervals. During his early years, when his mother had always a baby on hand, he was the special charge of his grandmother. Though the red hair rather existed in Max's imagination, Herman had inherited the quick, passionate temper of the Steiners. He was morbidly sensitive, morbidly excitable and enthusiastic, and in his affections was a little volcano.

Pride, however, made him conceal what he felt, as much as possible, but volcanoes will have their eruptions. And there were times when he poured out his love upon his mother and his grandmother in a way that almost frightened them. Otherwise he was truthfulness personified, and conscientious to the last degree.

Max did not understand or know how to manage him. He found him awkward with his hands, unlucky with his footsteps and dull with his brain. For Herman did nothing he was taught to do in the right way; was continually falling down and stumbling about, and could not learn the clock, even under the persuasive influence of the rod. There did not seem to be much promise that the child would ever make a successful carpenter, and therefore Max was dissatisfied with him.

Doris, on the other hand, loved him for the very eagerness and enthusiasm that made him so often get into trouble. She was sorry for him that his temper was so passionate, because she saw the shame and pain it caused him. She would not believe he was dull, but she could not give any reason for her opinion, except that he looked as bright as other children. And she always wound up with the mental conclusion:

"At any rate, he loves me so!"

The grandmother took advantage of his ardent temperament, and trained him to be a most religious child. She talked to him about his dear Lord and Master till he caught the glow and fervor of her affections. She made him feel that nothing is too much to do or to suffer for Christ Jesus our Savior, so that if he had lived in the days of persecution, he would have gone, a radiant little martyr, straight to the stake.

Max's nearest neighbors, were the Goschens, who had a son not far from Herman's age. He was a good-natured, mischievous fellow, and the two boys were naturally thrown together at school—and, by the way, Max made Herman shrink from Kurt with a certain aversion, by continually holding him up to him as the model by which he would have him shape his life.

"Don't get into such a passion! Neighbor's boy Kurt never does."

"Chop the wood faster! Neighbor's boy Kurt does it twice as fast."

"What will you make of our Herman?" Doris one night asked Max, when, after displaying more than usual inaptitude for what his father wished him to do, the boy had gone, with flushed cheeks and tearful eyes, to bed.

"I don't really know," said Max, "I never saw such a boy in my life. But of course I must teach him my own trade."

"But will he ever learn it?"

"He must learn."

"Our Minna is very different from Herman," said Doris, "already she is of great use to me. And Bernhard will perhaps be less troublesome than Herman."

"As to that, he is coming on in much the say way as his brother."

"People say he is so handsome," said Doris.

The words carried Max back to the days of his courtship and marriage when he had regarded Doris as such a pretty girl.

"I will admit that he looks like you," he conceded. "Do you know, Doris, I have been looking over my account book, and find things look very well? There is Han Goschen drinking himself to death and spending as fast as he earns. Think, how you came near marrying that fellow."

"Indeed, that is not true!" cried Doris.

"Well, he came near marrying you, then, only you had your objections. As to Herman, a carpenter he surely shall be."

"If there was anything else he could learn easier," suggested Doris.

"Yes, you would make a regular girl of him if I would permit," said Max. "But I will not permit it! The moment he is old enough to be of use to me, I shall take him from school and set him to work. He shall clean the stable, on that you may depend. He shall cut short fodder for the cattle, morning and night. He shall collect our fuel, and make our fires. Yes, my boys shall do as did their fathers before them."

Doris dared say no more. She went silently on with her spinning, oppressed with anxiety, yet not knowing what better could be done for Herman than all his father proposed to do.

After a time she ventured to ask:

"Shall you buy more cattle at the market to-morrow?"

"Why not?" returned Max.

There was no more said that night, and long before daybreak Max was up and away.

The children studied their lessons as usual from four o'clock till six, and then each had its own business to attend to. Herman must look after the cattle, and cut short fodder for them, and put fresh water into the drinking trough. Little Minna helped her mother to sweep the house, to arrange the breakfast table, and to wash the dishes. She was a fair-haired, veritable little woman, always composed and quiet, and young as she was, a real helper within doors and without. Bernhard was to look after the hens and the geese and little Adolph, and his office was one of no small life and stir.

By the time they would set off for school, everything was in perfect order, and Doris was ready to sit down to spin, and the old grandmother to take her knitting and go to her beloved seat under the linden tree. Herman and Minna were to knit all the way to school, for the walk was long. Each carried a little basket on the arm, to hold the ball of yarn, and the slice of bread and the baked apple which were to serve as their lunch.

"Do you know, Herman," said Minna, "that last night, after we were in bed, the dear grandmother wound our yarn on a bit of money? Yes, really and truly on a silver piece!"

"No!" said Herman incredulously.

"Yes, really and truly. Mother was saying that our stockings grew so slowly, and grandmother laughed, and said that winding the yarn on a bit of money made the stocking grow faster."

"How could it?" asked Herman.

"Why, don't you see that we shall be in such a hurry to get at our money that we shall knit day and night?"

"Pooh! I shan't," said Herman. "I hate to knit. I wish I lived in a country where only women and girls knit the stockings."

"Is there such a country?" asked Minna.

"To be sure there is. Look here, Minna. Isn't this flower pretty?"

"Yes, I suppose so," replied Minna, rather indifferently.

"Here are some more, quite different. Look, this is beautiful."

"Don't keep asking me to look," said Minna. "I am setting the heel of my stocking, and counting the stitches."

"How nice it is to have father gone all day!" said Herman.

"It's very naughty to say that," Minna felt constrained to say, though it obliged her to recount her stitches.

Herman wondered if it was really naughty, and one thought leading to another, he was silent until they reached the door of the school.

3

The children acquitted themselves as they usually did at school. Minna repeated her lessons with perfect accuracy, word for word. Her cool and quiet mind applied itself without let or hindrance to the task before it, and all her sums came right, and all her work was well done. Herman, if allowed to repeat his lessons in his own words, would have done well also. But the teacher required the exact words of the text, and it was next to impossible for the child to commit words to memory. He was sent back to his seat in disgrace, feeling guilty and ashamed, aware that all the other children were laughing at him, and puzzled to know how he happened to be so stupid and all the other children so clever. When it came to the writing lesson, things were no better. He got the ink all over his hands and blotted every page. The teacher took him by the shoulder, shook him soundly, and declared that he never would learn to write. The neighbor's boy Kurt pinched him slyly, and made him start suddenly and upset his inkstand. Another shaking from the teacher followed swiftly. Herman cried with shame and anger, and wiped away his tears with his inky hands till he made a perfect fright of himself. But he was used to being miserable, and to getting over it, so when school was done, and they all went scampering homeward, he recovered his spirits, and laughed and ran and shouted as merrily as the rest, though with less of their thoughtless lightheartedness. The sufferings of children are as real as those of their elders, but how much more easily they are replaced by passing joys!

Doris was sitting under the linden tree, with her mother, when the boys reached home.

"Has father come home?" was the first question, and on learning that he had not, they threw themselves and their satchels on the ground at their mother's feet, with a sense of rest and comfort that the long walk and the fatigue of school made very pleasant.

"Mother," said Herman, "I wish I had something alive to love. I haven't anything but Minchen, and she isn't my own cat, but Minna's."

"Am I, then, not alive?" asked Doris, laughing.

Herman jumped up and threw his arms around her neck for his answer.

"You hurt me, Herman," she said. "Is it always necessary to choke people because you love them?"

Herman blushed and darted away. It was many a day before his mother got another such embrace.

He threw himself upon the ground again, and lay a long time silent. The scene on which he gazed with some latent sense of its majesty and beauty was made up of snowcapped mountains, green valleys, pine forests, and quaint little cottages almost hidden by the fruit trees with which they were encompassed. Nothing was lacking to its perfection but the peaceful groups of cattle grazing on hillside and plain, which with us are one of the elements in every rural scene. What would one of our cows think had happened to her, should she suddenly find herself shut out from the free air of heaven, to pass her life in seclusion, like a pet bird in its cage, as do her foreign relatives?

"Mother," said Herman when he had recovered from her little rebuke, "what is it that makes people feel like crying when they look at mountains and such things?"

"As if they ever did!" returned his mother absently.

"Well, but they do, mother," persisted Herman.

"Then I suppose they're homesick," she said.

"How can they be homesick when they're always at home?" urged Herman.

"I can't imagine what you are talking about," said Doris. "But let me ask you one question. Have you cut the short fodder for the cow?"

Herman started up, looking alarmed and guilty.

"Will father soon be here?" he asked anxiously.

At that moment a boy not much older than himself appeared, leading a white calf by a cord.

"Here comes neighbor's boy Kurt," said Doris. "He has been to meet his father. They must be close at hand. Run, Herman, and get to the stable at once."

Herman ran, but the white calf was too much for him to resist. He stopped to pat it, and begged the privilege of leading it a little way.

"It is my own," said Kurt. "Bought with my own money. Isn't it a big, strong fellow?"

"It's a beauty," said Herman, and he knelt down and pressed his cheek to its pure white face.

Never had the word money meant anything to him before. But now it meant a beautiful, soft, living creature to feed, to caress, to love and to live in a little stable built by his own hands! That stocking must be finished, and grandmother must wind him another ball of yarn!

He felt such delight when he saw the docile creature follow him, that he could not find for it enough endearing names.

"You are a regular bossy calf yourself," said Kurt, laughing. "I would think you were talking to your sweetheart."

Herman blushed, and took care to say no more. Suddenly it flashed across his mind that he had not yet attended to the cow. He darted off once more in the direction of the stable, where his father received him with a box on the ear that would have knocked him down, had not another on the opposite ear restored the balance. He resented the blow, yet dared not show his anger.

"I did not mean to disobey, father," he said, "but I just stopped to look at neighbor's boy Kurt, who has a white calf of his own."

"You're a white calf yourself," was the answer. "All you are fit for is to have a rope tied round your neck, and to be led through the village for people to look at."

"Yes, father," said Herman, now thoroughly humbled. He felt that he must indeed be a calf who had been called so twice within ten minutes. He fell to cutting the fodder as fast as he could, but his eyes were full of tears, and he cut his fingers again and again. His father had brought home another cow, and Doris and her mother, and all the children, came out to see it. Little Adolph was made to pat the newcomer with his fat hand, and to bid her welcome. He held in his arms a remarkable wooden horse, which Max had brought from the fair. It possessed a rampant tail of an uncompromising character, and was adorned with a hen's feather in its head, to give it a military air.

They were soon seated around the supper table, where Max appeared in unusual spirits, and had much to tell about the sayings and doings of the fair. Evidently it had been a prosperous day with him, for instead of working all the evening, he wrote in his account book with an air of satisfaction.

"I shall buy a bit more land tomorrow," he said to Doris. "Things are looking very well. We shall have more fruit than we shall know what to do with in the autumn, and I have arranged to exchange a part of it for meal. And you will soon finish your fifty yards of linen, and linen, in these times, is pure gold."

All he had in his head Max had now spoken out. Making money and sparing money was to his mind the chief end of man. As for his harsh ways with his children, he never dreamed of their not being the perfection of good management.

Poor Herman! He who might literally have been led by the silken thread of love and kindness, was driven by brute force well-nigh to desperation.

"There were no pinecones for lighting the fire

this morning," said Doris.

"The children must bring some more cones, then," said Max. "Send them before school."

Herman and Bernhard exchanged glances of dismay.

"Then may we learn our lessons tonight, father?" asked Herman.

"No," said Max. "You should not have let your mother run out of cones."

"It was my fault," said Doris. "I just didn't notice that the supply was so low."

The boys, therefore, worked at toy making, under their father's eye, all the evening. Their hearts were heavy, and their hands awkward, and Doris sat painfully at her wheel, listening to all that went on, and wondering why her children were so slow to learn, when in many things they seemed so bright and full of life and energy.

The next morning she whispered to the children to take their books with them when they went to the forest.

"Once there," she said, "gather the cones with all your might, then sit down and study in the same way. I cannot bear to think of your all being chastised at school."

The children set off with light hearts, and under the stimulus of the excitement of studying in such hot haste, Herman learned his lessons well, and for once received a gracious word from the schoolteacher.

On their return from school they were all set for gathering fruit. They had quantities of plums which they helped their mother to spread in the sun to dry.

"It is almost time for the long vacation," said Minna. "Then we shall not have to go to school, and can help mother so much more."

The long autumnal vacation was Herman's special aversion. The object of it was to give the children of the peasantry time to help in the harvest time. The lower classes had to glean in the fields of the more prosperous neighbors, with bags suspended from their necks, and there was every variety of work to do in preparation for the winter.

Herman was thus brought into contact with his father almost constantly, and had ample opportunity to display his impractical character to the utmost extent.

4

"What are you idling here for?" cried Max, coming suddenly upon Herman, as with book in hand, he sat under the linden tree on the first day of vacation.

"I was not idling, father. I was reading," he replied.

"And what's the use of reading? Does it bring cows into the stable, or meat into the sack?"

As Herman could not maintain that either of these results naturally flowed from books, he remained speechless.

The look of distress and perplexity in the boy's

face somewhat touched his father's heart, and he said in a milder tone:

"Books are for the rich, not for the poor. We must have moss collected for the cow's bedding. Go ask your mother for the bags, and set off at once."

"Is Bernhard to go, too?" asked Herman.

"Certainly."

The boys set off on a brisk trot, like two young ponies, and soon had to stop to take a breath.

"Do you know what I'm going to do?" asked Herman. "I've got a book at the bottom of the bag, and you shall collect the moss while I read to you."

"But that will make us get home late, and then what will father say?"

"I suppose he'll box our ears. I don't know how yours are, but mine have gotten quite used to it by now."

"But what will you do about it when you say your prayers tonight?"

"Well, I don't know. Do you suppose the dear Lord isn't willing that we should read a little bit?"

"But father thinks we are at work, and it would be cheating for one of us to be reading."

"Yes, I suppose it would. So here goes!" And Herman threw himself down, and began to scramble up the moss and to tumble it into the bag with nervous haste and energy.

"We'll work fast, and save a little time for our

book," said Herman. "But look here, Bernhard. Some of this moss is so pretty. Do you suppose all the dear Lord made it for was for old cows to sleep on?"

"I don't know," said Bernhard. "If we could get time, we might find out in some book. But we never shall get time."

"I'll tell you what I read somewhere, once. There are some large cities, not very far from here, where men sit in their houses all day, reading. They get so that they know almost everything. Now, if I was rich, I could do the same. Then I would not be forever tumbling about, and hurting myself, and tearing and wearing out my clothes, and father wouldn't be scolding, and, Bernhard, you could do the same. For next to me, father scolds you the most."

"Yes," said Bernhard, sighing. "Take care, Herman!"

But the warning came too late. In the ardor of his talk, Herman had left his work and climbed a high rock which was covered with moss, and very slippery, and climbing with him always ended in a fall. He lay now upon the ground, bruised and sore.

"Oh, dear!" he cried. "How am I ever to get home?"

"Are you hurt so dreadfully?" asked Bernhard, beginning to cry.

"It isn't the hurt I mind," answered Herman

sharply. "But don't you see my clothes, how they have split to pieces? You needn't go to talking as if I minded getting hurt, when you know all I care about is father's scolding me so!"

But in an instant, seeing Bernhard's color change, he was ashamed of having spoken so impatiently.

"I didn't mean to say anything to plague you," he said, "only when I think how angry father will be, I don't know what I'm about."

"It's no matter," said Bernhard. "Perhaps mother won't tell father."

"She'll have to tell him. Else how am I to get new clothes?"

Dragging their bags of moss after them, the boys walked sadly homeward.

On seeing the plight he was in, Doris laid down the potato she was peeling, in order to clasp her hands with horror.

"What will the dear father say?" she cried. "And it is such an unlucky moment, too, for he is just a little out of sorts. And he is so seldom out of sorts! Oh, Herman!" she added with tears in her eyes, "how can you be willing to give me so much trouble? Don't you know that it hurts me more to have you punished than it would to be punished myself?"

This was a new view of things to Herman. He immediately rushed out to the little shed at the end of the house where his father was at work.

"Father!" he cried, "you may do anything to me you've a mind to, only don't let dear mother know. You may beat me or knock me down and kick me—I don't care how much it hurts—only please, father, please don't let mother know!"

Alas for the child born and bred among the coarse natures nurtured in the rough wilds of the Black Forest!

What punishment Max, in his anger, inflicted on the generous child was never known save by the father who dealt the blows and the boy who bore them in silence, lest mother should hear.

When it was all over, and Herman went back to the house, he instinctively crept to his grandmother for refuge. He did not think, but he felt, that she would have more courage to bear the sight of him than his mother could, not because she loved him less, but because she always bore up so well in times of trouble.

"Do you think I might put on my Sunday clothes?" he whispered to her.

"Who tore these?"

"I did, partly."

"And who else?"

"Father did, a little," replied Herman. His grandmother rose and sought for the Sunday clothes.

"I know a boy who has more reason at this moment to feel unhappy than even you, dear Herman," she said. "Do you know our neighbor

Herr Goschen has just been carried past the house, dead? And the last words his Kurt spoke to him were angry words."

Herman shuddered. He resolved never to speak an angry word to anyone he loved, as long as he lived.

"I'd rather father would live, and whip me," he said.

"Especially if the whipping is for your good," said his grandmother. "And now go out to your father, and tell him what has happened."

Max was greatly shocked to hear what had befallen his neighbor. He hurried out to learn the particulars of this sudden death, and when he came back was so quiet and subdued that Doris ventured to tell him that Herman must have new clothes.

5

For a time there was a lull in the tempest. Max was less severe, and the children more attentive. Among them all, incredible deeds were done by way of preparation for the winter, and the long vacation, when it came to a close, found them surrounded with many comforts. Doris felt concerned for Babele Goschen, for whom she had a certain friendship, growing out of the fact that they had always been neighbors, rather than from any point of sympathy with her.

Babele, however, boasted that she was no

sooner down than she was upon her feet again. It was truly a sad thing to lose one's husband, but luckily there were only two children to feed, and they were even now beginning to spare and to earn. She came, a few weeks after the death of Hans, to spend the evening with Doris.

Max sat on a bench and appeared to be asleep, his ears were open, however, though his eyes were shut.

"Well, neighbor," Babele began, "have you got quite ready for the winter? They say it is to be a very bitter one."

"We have yet a pig to kill and to care for," said Doris. "And my Herman has yet some fuel to collect."

"You should see my winter stores," said Babele. "There is no reason we should starve because the father is not here to eat with us. He never could wish such a piece of folly as that. I have laid in plenty of fuel, and of plums and other dried fruit, and of meal, we shall have no lack. We have hay for the cattle, and corn for the hens and the geese. My Kurt makes me almost forget that I have no husband. He thinks of everything and attends to everything like a man. Next news, he will be sitting at the tavern, and drinking his beer on holidays as his father did before him."

"My Herman is a good, kind boy," said Doris.

"My Kurt," continued Babele, "is born with a natural gift for a bargain. I must tell you how he has managed to trade off potatoes and plums for a big, likely calf. Ha! ha! He'll make his way in the world!"

"My Bernhard takes the whole care of little Adolph," said Doris. "When the child is with Bernhard, I need never give him a thought."

"And there's my Lizette," pursued Babele, "she already beats me at spinning. You must see her chest of linen. Upon my word, whoever gets her for a wife will find her well clothed, to say the least of it. Not to speak of the four silver spoons inherited by her from our relative the Baumeisterin. For we have highbred people as our kin, you know."

"Yes," said Doris, pursuing also the thread of her discourse, "and my Minna is a discreet little maiden who never gives me a care. If you will believe it, she has today made a pie almost entirely with her own hands. You shall see it with your own eyes." And Doris displayed a pie a foot and a half wide, filled with plums, split open, the open side being uppermost, and presenting an attractive appearance.

"The question is, is the pie fit to eat?" cried neighbor Goschen. "Who could believe that such a child could make a pie one could tolerate?"

This crafty speech had its desired effect. Doris ran for a knife and a plate, and cut the pie in eager haste, even forgetting to look at Max to see if he were really asleep.

The complaisant neighbor devoured a generous portion.

"I can't exactly say what was left out in the making," she said. "Spice, I think. I can tell better after trying another piece. Nay, I believe it is the
sugar the child has forgotten. Well, to oblige you
I will force down yet a third morsel, though I
could not do it for a stranger. Let me see, it is
not the sugar after all, it is actually too sweet. Yes,
the pie, for a beginner, will do extremely well.
The crust being tough, and there not being
enough sugar, I mean there being too much
sugar, are things of no great consequence after
all. But if one really wants to see pie that is abso-
lutely a miracle, one should see my Lizette's."

At this juncture Max saw fit to awaken, and to
took with displeasure at the enormous hole
neighbor Goschen had made in the pie intended
for his supper.

"We shall drop in and get a taste of Lizette's
pie," he said dryly.

"Do, neighbor. And at the same time you shall
see our pig. The very finest in all the Black Forest, you may be sure. Doris, I'll try yet another
morsel of your Minna's pie, just to give the child
a pleasure. And if you will some day send her to
my house, Lizette shall teach her how to make
one that is really eatable."

By this time Doris was subdued to the degree
that she had no more to say about her children,

and Babele Goschen thereafter pursued her discourse without interruption.

As soon as she had gone, Max was magnani-
mous enough to say to Doris, while he bestowed
upon her his highest mark of friendship, namely,
a good slap upon her shoulders:

"Thank heaven that I married you instead of
that chattering magpie."

"But think how much she gets out of her children," said Doris.

"That is true. But one can't have everything in
a wife," said Max regretfully.

The vacation being over, the children went
back to school, and little Adolph was thrown now
entirely on his mother's hands. His grandmother
was very feeble at this time and suffering greatly
with rheumatism. While Doris was busy with her
household affairs, therefore, Adolph was equally
busy in getting into every conceivable kind of
mischief.

On coming home from school the first day, and
inquiring for his little charge, Bernhard was in-
formed that Adolph had been missing for more
than half an hour.

"He has not gone out of doors, has he mother?"

"Oh! no," replied Doris. "He is safe somewhere,
and if he knew I was about to make knoepfles
for supper, I am sure he would come out from
his hiding place."

And sure enough, there immediately emerged

from beneath the bed a little figure on all fours, with tangled hair, adorned with five knitting needles, and arms, legs, and body involved in a maze of blue yarn.

"If Adolph hasn't gone and raveled out my stocking!" cried Herman. "My very stocking that was almost done! And Minna said grandmother wound my ball on a piece of money! Adolph! what have you done with the money?"

Adolph cast his eyes downward, and looked steadfastly at his left hand, which was doubled firmly over the little silver piece.

At this moment Max entered. Adolph knew enough, on seeing his father, to behave with propriety on the instant, and dropped the money immediately.

"Where did the child get that money?" asked Max with displeasure.

The children all began to explain together.

As soon as he understood the case, Max tossed the money into the grandmother's lap.

"It is quite enough for Doris to spoil the children," he said, "without getting others to help her."

No one dared to say a word. Minna patiently disentangled Adolph from his net, and wound the yarn on a bit of paper. Herman had now all his work to do over, without the agreeable prospect of finding his labor rewarded when his task was done. He felt reckless and disgusted. All the evening he showed that he felt so, and Max at last sent him to bed in disgrace.

Thus everything fell back into the old way, each day alienating the boy more and more from his father, and making Max more and more severe and unreasonable.

The winter was one of unusual rigor, and it was necessary to use more fuel than ever before.

6

One night after the children were in bed, Max sat looking over his account book in a morose way, and at length he said:

"I'll tell you what it is, Doris, it is time that boy left school and came to help me in my work. I have more orders than I can fill. The Herr Pastor has waited for his new table already three weeks, and there are also many other persons clamoring for work that must be done. I need help, and help I must have."

"He is very young to leave school," said Doris.

"That is of no consequence. He can read and

write, and add and divide. What else is there to learn? And, at any rate, he never would make a scholar, for the schoolteacher says he is a dull boy—the very dullest in school. I wonder what I have done that I must be the father of such a good-for-nothing?"

Doris dared make no answer. To hide her tears, she went to see if the children were well covered in their little beds.

Herman was wide awake, and his glittering eyes showed that he had heard what had passed between them.

"Oh, mother!" he whispered, throwing his arms about her, "why did our dear Lord make such a good-for-nothing?"

"Hush, dear Herman, I can't talk to you now. Go to sleep like a good boy."

"I am not a good boy, and I can't get to sleep," he answered.

"What's all that noise when I'm casting up accounts?" cried Max. "Ha! I wish I had been taught the addition table when I was a boy. There's no great fun in counting on one's fingers with half a dozen people talking, and putting you out."

"I don't think Herman has learned it yet," said Doris, catching eagerly at this straw. "You surely will not take him from school until he has done so, seeing how bad it is not to know it?"

"He shall learn it at home," said Max, "I'll begin with him tomorrow. Or no, tomorrow I must go up the mountain after fuel. Seems to me you burn a great deal more than you need, Doris."

"I will try to be more careful," she said. "And Max, won't you let me teach Herman his math tables? You know how hard it is for him to commit to memory, and how he tries your patience. And dear Max, don't be angry with me, but perhaps you don't notice how afraid he is of you, and how many blunders he makes because he is in such terror."

"There's no use in arguing with me," replied Max. "The boy is the plague of my life, and always will be; but I cannot leave him to you to be petted and spoiled. If anybody can beat a thing into his head, I can, and if worst comes to worst, I will set him to watching the geese."

"Nay, you never will degrade him to that extent!" cried Doris.

"Yes, a goose-boy he shall be, unless he improves!" cried Max. "And tomorrow, at any rate, he shall not go to school. I must have him and Bernhard help me on the mountain tomorrow."

"Would you let me go in their place?"

"No," he answered, "and twice over, no I say! It will do for the Herr Pastor to tell me once that I let my wife work too hard for one in her station. I don't care to hear the same tune twice."

There was no more to be said. And Doris could not help feeling a little relieved, since it must be so, that Herman was to leave school, for getting his lessons was such a painful, laborious process for him. And then if he was so dull, as the teacher declared he was, what was the use of trying to make him learn?

But with her true motherly instincts she felt that he was not dull, and her heart yearned over him with fresh love and sympathy.

Herman slept little that night, for he now felt thoroughly degraded and heart broken. Neither could he force down the breakfast he needed before encountering the cold and fatigue before him.

Doris watched for a moment in which to speak a tender word to him.

"Don't be cast down, dear child," she said. "Perhaps our dear Lord knows of something you can do well, and when the time comes will let you know what it is. Meanwhile try to be a good boy, and vex the dear father as little as possible, you know he is so seldom vexed."

"Oh! I do wish we were not so poor," said Herman.

"Poor! who says we are poor?" cried Doris, clasping her hands in amazement, "who says we are poor?"

"But do rich people go out to collect fuel?"

"Herman!" said Doris, trying now to be severe, "is it possible that you are a lazy boy?"

"I'm afraid I am," said Herman. "But are people who sit all day, reading and writing, lazy? Because

I have read of wise men who did nothing else, and I would like to be a wise man."

"Never let the dear father hear such wild words fall from your lips!" cried Doris. "The dear father places thriftiness before all things."

There was silence for a time, and Herman chopped the sticks on which he was at work, with a vague desire to unburden himself to his mother, yet not knowing how.

"As soon as I get old enough I'll go away somewhere," he said desperately.

Little Minna, washing the breakfast cups, would gladly have clasped her hands at this audacious speech, but they were too full. She therefore suppressed her emotions and washed faithfully on.

Doris shook her head in silence, but she said to herself:

"If Max drives my children away from me, I had better die than live."

"Come, boys, it is time to go," said Max, hurrying in.

"Have you our dinner ready, Doris? For we shall not be back till night."

"Yes, here is coffee, and here are bread and potatoes. You will roast the potatoes and warm the coffee?" she asked.

"Yes, never fear. Bring along the cords, children."

Doris had just time to thrust a bit of cake into

Herman's pocket, and they were off. The village was soon left behind them. Then the little river that traversed it was crossed on a footbridge, and presently a narrow, winding path began to lead them up the side of the mountain. They walked on in single file, without a word, the only variety to the silent progress being an occasional fall, the path being slippery at this season of the year. Herman's heart felt like lead. It seemed to him that even his mother was beginning to lose sympathy with him. The thought of being taken from school and made into a mere goose-boy tortured him. If possible, it seemed worse to him now that he was bounding up the mountain side, invigorated by the breeze, than it did when he lay wearied and discouraged on his little bed last night.

Besides, the anguish then suppressed lest his father should hear, must have vent. He lingered a little behind the rest, then darting in among the leafless bushes that skirted the path, he threw himself upon the ground and burst into passionate tears and groans.

"I'm just a good-for-nothing! A good-for-nothing!" he said to himself over and over again. And then, when he had spent himself with crying, he looked up to the blue sky above him, and it had for him an air of friendliness, and there seemed to be a certain peace in the very silence and repose of nature. He folded his hands, and said, out of the very depths of his heart:

"Oh, dear Lord! can't You help me not to be a good-for-nothing?"

And then he remembered that it was wrong to idle away the time when he ought to be at work, and he started to his feet and began to ascend the mountain with hasty steps. As he pressed on, he wondered that he did not overtake his father, nor hear his voice. Was it possible that he had taken the wrong path? He stopped, and shouted with all his might, but there was no answer, and the silence that just now seemed so soothing appalled and oppressed him. The truth was that, worn out by the sleepless and sorrowful night he had passed, and relieved by the tears he had shed, the child had actually fallen asleep for a few moments, thus giving the others time to get out of sight and hearing. Then, in his haste, and only too much in accordance with his past habits, he had chosen the wrong path, and was every moment going further and further astray. Unconscious of having slept, he felt sure of soon overtaking his father, and of making up for lost time by unusual diligence. But after a while he began to feel some misgivings. He knew that to get lost in the mountains was the easiest thing in the world. He knew he would begin to suffer with hunger, and, as night came on, with cold, but, above all, he knew that his father would be angry—oh, how angry! and, if he should perish and never he heard of again, would perhaps feel it a mercy to be rid of him. But then his mother! Wouldn't she mourn for her poor lost boy? Wouldn't Bernhard, who loved him so much, cry himself to sleep that night? Wouldn't even Minna, whom nothing ever seemed to trouble, be sorry if he never came back?

He was not a timid boy, and after a few moments of perplexity, he resolved to retrace his steps, and see if he could not find another path. He ate half the cake his mother had given him, as soon as he began to feel hungry, but saved half for Bernhard.

Meanwhile, Max was venting his anger at the disappearance of the boy by slashing at the trees right and left. As fast as boughs and branches fell, Bernhard made them up into large bundles, and tied them together with cords. It was hard work for such a little fellow, but he dared not complain. Max had no doubt that Herman was hiding somewhere to escape this task. Bernhard did not know what to think, but never for one moment suspected his brother of so disgraceful an act. As the day advanced, Max stopped his work for a time and made a little fire, when the coffee was warmed and the potatoes were roasted. As Bernhard sat dipping his bread into his coffee, he thought anxiously of Herman, and ventured, for the first time, to break the silence that had prevailed for so many hours.

"Father," he said, "may I go down the path a little way, and see if I can find Herman? Perhaps he has had a fall, and can't get up."

"No," replied Max sternly.

Bernhard dared say no more, but he worked thereafter with a distracted mind, listening every few moments in hope of hearing Herman's voice, and doing what he had to do wearily and without heart. When at last it was time to go, Max placed a bundle of sticks upon Bernhard's head, took a second on his own, and the remaining ones were sent rolling and bounding down the pathway that led homeward. They reached the house just at nightfall, and everybody came out to meet and to relieve them.

"Why, where's Herman?" cried Doris.

Max was in too sullen a mood to answer.

"Haven't you seen him, mother?" asked Bernhard. "Oh, mother! then he's lost! he's lost!" And Bernhard threw himself into her arms with a cry of anguish that went even to his father's heart.

"Do you mean to tell me that you have left my Herman to perish on the mountain?" said Doris in a hoarse voice, and confronting Max, who recoiled before her, and was still speechless.

But when he found his voice, that was hoarse too.

"Get the lantern," he said.

Everybody was bewildered, and ran everywhere

looking for it. Max found it himself, lighted it, and plunged out into the darkness. After a moment, hearing sobs and footsteps behind him, he turned and saw Doris and Bernhard following him.

"Go back, both of you!" he said. "The neighbors will help me, but you will be in the way. Go back, I say!"

If they had withstood him, he would have felled them to the earth. They went back, and Bernhard told over and over again all there was to tell, till at last, worn out with crying, he was made to go to bed with the other children.

"You must go too, mother," said Doris.

"I cannot, dear," she replied.

7

So they sat, these two, through the long hours; the grandmother weeping silently, and with hands folded in prayer; Doris with fevered cheeks and parched lips, and hands and feet of ice. There had been friction on the wheels of her domestic life. She had had her little cares, and vexations, and trials, but a real sorrow she had never known. And now, in the twinkling of an eye, this awful calamity had come upon her! Her mind traveled back over the whole history of her child. She recalled all his infantine graces, all the lovely ways of his childhood, all the intense and passionate love his boyhood had lavished on her. And all this was gone forever!

She walked to and fro in the room, and asked herself if a good God could let such things happen.

"Mother!" she cried at last, "I am getting bewildered. Tell me, is God good when He does such terrible things to us?"

"All my children, save you, dear, lie in God's earth. And your father—you know he was snatched from me in one awful moment, when I was but young, as you are now, my Doris. But what then? God never was anything but good."

Doris shook her head, and walked yet once more up and down the room.

"You are too tired to find comfort even in Him," said her mother. "If you could only sleep, if but for a moment!"

"I wish you would go to bed, mother. You know I cannot. Tell me once more, mother, are you sure God is good?"

Again thus solemnly adjured, the poor feeble mother burst into tears. She held out her arms, and Doris ran into their shelter, just as she had done when a child.

"Whatever He does, He is good," said the mother. "But I believe He means to save Herman."

"Oh, mother! He must save him! Have you told Him so? Have you asked Him?"

"Nay, my Doris, we may not say 'must' to our dear Lord. Surely, we can trust Herman to Him?"

In her distress, Doris withdrew herself from her mother's arms, and went and knelt down by the side of her bed and tried to pray. But her tongue seemed to cling to the roof of her mouth. Yet the unuttered prayer was heard and answered, and she rose from her knees, comforted and cheered.

"I will make coffee for dear mother," she said to herself, "and have some ready for Max when he comes. Poor Max! he must be so tired!"

She prepared the coffee, and made soup. Yet she dared not say to herself that either were for Herman.

These little womanly tasks beguiled her of a portion of the weary time, and then she saw that her mother had, at last, fallen asleep in her chair. She wrapped a shawl carefully about her, and sitting down on the bench by the table, laid her aching head upon it. God gave her, as she sat there, a few moments sleep, though she never knew it. How manifold are the gifts from His lavish hand which we receive in like unconsciousness and for which we never thank Him!

At daybreak she was startled by a footstep, and with a beating heart, sprang to her feet. It was Babele Goschen, come on a visit of condolence.

"They haven't found him?" she asked. "Well, I didn't expect they had. Bless me, you look as if

you had a burning fever! And the dear old
mother looks pale and tired. Ah! you should not
have made her sit up with you. You should have
made her go to bed. You remember the time my
Kurt got so dreadfully burned? I was young then,
and couldn't keep awake, and my mother sat up
with him night after night. And she never held
up her head from that time until her death. Well!
the old must die, and a few years more or less
can't make much difference to them."

"It would make a great deal of difference to me
if I should lose *my* mother," said Doris. "But, oh,
neighbor! What do you think? Will they find my
Herman?"

"Well, as I was saying to my children, these boys
who are always woolgathering are sure to come
to harm. Your Herman never seemed quite to
have his wits about him. Such a child needs a
sound beating every night at bed time. I cannot
imagine how he went to work to get lost. My children never get lost. What makes yours, do you
suppose?"

"Not one of them was ever lost before," said
Doris. "Oh, Babele! Can't you say something to
comfort me?"

"Of course. That's what I came for. But it does
puzzle me to see children so different from
mine."

"But, oh! Do you think they will find him?" repeated Doris.

"It depends on where he is," replied Babele. "If the child keeps wandering on, he will very likely be getting further and further away. And besides, groping about in the dark, he would be likely to get dreadful falls. If he should fall into one of those deep chasms, there wouldn't be enough of him left to be worth bringing home. And then again, if he does keep stiff, he'd perish with the cold. Last night was bitterly cold. Even our cows were restless, and so were our pigs, and my Kurt had to get up and pacify his white calf, it was so uneasy. Besides, the child would soon begin to suffer with hunger. I don't know exactly how long it takes to starve to death, but they say it's an awful way to die. And then again—but what are you doing? You are not listening in the least! I was going to say that sometimes the wolves—"

Doris had risen in a frantic way, and arrayed herself in her outer garments. She had brought forth blankets and placed them in a basket, with coffee and soup and wine. She now proceeded to awaken Minna, who still slept profoundly.

"Keep up the fire," she whispered, "and if the dear father comes home, see that his breakfast is hot."

"Why, where are you going?" cried Babele, rising and looking with amazement at Doris.

"Where should I go, if the mother's heart in me can ever beat again after the terrible things you have been saying?" cried Doris, turning fiercely upon her guest. And in another moment she was gone. Babele lifted up her hands and slowly followed her.

"Well!" she said to herself, with a long breath, "I never was faced by a tigress or a she wolf, but I rather think I know now how it would seem. And this is what one gets for leaving one's warm bed to speak a word of comfort to a fellow creature!"

She moved slowly homeward, while Doris sped panting on her way. She was crossing the footbridge, when she was confronted by Max. He looked jaded and dejected.

"Where are you going, Doris?" he cried.

"To find my Herman'" she answered, trying to pass him.

"You must not go," he answered. "I am only returning to seek more help, and shall continue the search as long as there is any hope."

"And how long will that be?"

Max turned away from her searching look.

"God only knows!" he said solemnly. "But now, Doris, go home. All that can be done, I will do."

"I'll not go home," said Doris quietly. "Let me pass, Max."

"I cannot. You must go home."

"I will not. See, Max, I never in my life disobeyed you before, but now I must."

He made no answer but turned back toward the mountain, and Doris followed him.

"Here is coffee, Max," she said, as they reached the path by which they were to ascend.

He shook his head and pushed onward; then turning, he performed the first act of gallantry that had adorned their married life, by transferring the basket from her head to his own. They went on in silence—Max leading the way, Doris following—till noonday, when both were exhausted.

"You must take some coffee, Max," said Doris. "There is no use in wasting your strength by fasting. Make a little fire and let me warm some for you. And here is soup, too."

Max threw himself wearily upon the ground and lighted the fire.

Doris warmed the soup and made him take some, and to please him drank some of the coffee herself. Then they sat a moment, each trying to read some hope and comfort in the face of the other. Suddenly Doris uttered a cry of joy.

"He has been here!" she cried. "Look, Max, here is a crumb of the cake I gave him yesterday. Come, let us take courage. Call to him, Max."

Max shouted, but in vain.

"We shall find him," said Doris eagerly.

"Let us go on. I feel courage, now that I know that he has been here. Oh, my Herman! If you could only know that we are near you!"

And she lifted up her voice and called him. For an instant there was the same awful silence as before; then came a faint cry, like the wail of a little child.

"Do you hear, Max?" said Doris, catching him by the arm. "Where does the sound come from?"

"Call again," said Max.

She called, and once more they heard the faint cry in answer.

Max listened as one bewildered.

"I cannot tell where the sound comes from," he said.

"It comes from some place a good way off, and below us," said Doris. "Can it be from this crevice? Oh, Max! If he is there, we never can get him out alive!"

Max threw himself at full length upon the ground, and cautiously looked over the edge. On a narrow ledge of projecting rock he saw the child lying motionless. That he was alive seemed little short of a miracle. He withdrew, still with caution, and blew a loud blast upon the horn that hung at his side.

"The men will soon come to help us now," he said to Doris. "With ropes I think we may be able to draw him up."

"But why doesn't he climb up?" cried Doris.

"He must be hurt," said Max. "I will go down and see. As soon as the men come up with the ropes, throw the end of one down to me."

"But isn't it dangerous?" asked Doris, with an involuntary shudder.

I suppose so. And, Doris, if I make a false step, and never come back, will you forgive me that I have been such a surly, ill-natured fellow?"

They clasped each other's hands silently, and without another word.

Doris sat down and hid her face in her hands. Dearly as she loved Herman, she felt now that Max was even dearer.

It seemed as if the men would never come. When they did, one of them, a stranger to Doris, volunteered to descend into the crevice. The others shrugged their shoulders and did not interfere.

Meanwhile, Max crept carefully down, knowing that one misstep would be certain destruction. But when he at last reached Herman, and found him lying on such a mere projection of the rock that the slightest motion would hurl him into the depths below, he could hardly suppress a cry of horror.

"How are you, my poor boy?" he asked, as soon as he caught Herman's eye.

"I didn't mean to do it, father," said Herman, "but I've broken my leg. Are you angry with me, father?" he added, not knowing how to interpret the expression on the face that was bending over him.

"Not I!" said Max. "But, Herman, if your leg is broken, I must have help in getting you out of this place. Do you think I can trust you not to move hand or foot while I go to fetch what I want? Or wait, I think I can put you where you will be safer, if you are willing to bear the pain."

Max spoke with love and tenderness, and Herman looked up at him with mute surprise.

"Oh, father!" he said with a sigh of relief, "I don't mind the pain when you talk like that!"

Just then a cheerful voice was heard, and a pair of legs came into view, speedily followed by the arms and head of the young stranger who had offered his services to Doris.

I am come to help you," he said, "is the child hurt? Ah! yes, I see!" he added, glancing at the pale face, so full of suppressed agony. "Keep up a good heart, my little fellow. We'll soon devise some way to get you to your mother. For mothers are the right thing when one gets hurt, aren't they?"

Herman tried to smile in answer, but he was in great pain and shivering with cold. Observing it, the young man climbed the ascent like a squirrel, and soon returned with one of the blankets. Of this they made a sort of hammock, and under the intelligent direction of their new friend, poor Herman was at last hoisted to the spot where his mother sat awaiting them.

"A little of the warm soup would refresh the poor fellow," said one of the men, glancing at the contents of the basket.

"Yes," cried Doris, "and there's coffee for all of

you. How could I forget it, when you had been seeking my boy all night!"

She knelt down by Herman and fed him with the soup, but he was in too much pain to speak to her. Now that he felt himself safe, he was more conscious of his sufferings, and longed to get home and to his own little bed. But it was a painful journey there, and he fainted more than once before he reached it. Then it was long before the doctor could be found, and when he came, he found the limb so swollen that it was impossible to set it at once. Thus the child's sufferings were prolonged. He was exhausted, too, by exposure and hunger, and for some days his case was very serious.

And now Max came out in a way that astonished everybody but himself, and became the most tender, the most faithful of nurses.

His perfect health enabled him to sit night after night by Herman's side, when even Doris was driven to bed by sheer exhaustion. And the tones of his rough voice became almost womanly in their tenderness as he tried to soothe the child's sufferings.

"Don't be so good to me, father," said Herman, "it makes me cry."

8

The young man who had been of such service to them on the mountain proved to be the new schoolteacher, who had come to supply the place of the old one, now too old for his position. He came every day to see Herman, at first from mere benevolence, but very soon he began to feel a peculiar interest in the patient little fellow.

"You bear the pain like a young hero," he said one day, when he was present at one of the doctor's visits.

"It worries mother if I cry out," said Herman.

"And you don't like to worry mother? That's a good boy," said the doctor.

"I ought to be good," said Herman timidly, "because I do not have as much sense as the other boys."

"What other boys?" asked the schoolteacher, with no little surprise.

"All the boys," said Herman.

"We shall see about that," said the schoolteacher, much amused, "as soon as you get well and come back to school. And now, suppose I read to you from a very entertaining book I have brought with me?"

Doris could hardly believe that the teacher would be so kind, and Herman was almost too much overwhelmed by the condescension to really enjoy it. But in a few moments he forgot his pain and everything else in the charm of the book. His eye kindled, his face flushed, and he felt like springing out of bed in his enthusiasm.

"This does not took like a lack of sense," thought the schoolteacher, as he glanced at the eager child.

"It won't do for me to read any more now," he said. "You are getting excited. I only wanted to make you forget the pain the doctor had caused you. Tomorrow I will come again and read a little more."

Herman thanked him, and lay back on his pillow, full of new thoughts which delighted him during many tiresome hours.

The next day when the schoolteacher came, he said:

"It will not be long before the doctor will let you employ your hands in some way, so as to pass away the time. What do you like to do best?"

"I don't like to tell," said Herman, "because it is something lazy."

"Ah, but just tell me! I'll never tell. Come and tell me!"

Herman smiled. How different this was from the old schoolteacher!

"Well," he said, with a long sigh, "I like to read the very best of anything. It must be because I am lazy. But I do try to learn to saw and plane and help father, and I do not know what makes me so clumsy. I never do anything well."

"Don't you suppose that if some boy should break his leg, you would know how to speak a cheering word to him? Then there would be one thing you could do well."

"Perhaps that's the reason our dear Lord let me break my leg," suggested Herman eagerly.

"Perhaps so. At any rate, you may be sure He did it for some good reason."

"Steiner," he said, entering the shed where Max was at work, "your boy needs encouraging. I cannot understand how it happens that he thinks so poorly of himself."

Max took off his cap and looked confused.

"The old schoolteacher told us he was a dull boy," he replied.

Now all this time no one had dared to ask Herman to admit how he had happened to get lost. Even his mother understood him so little as to dread hearing that he had willfully strayed away. One day, however, when he seemed strong enough to do so, she begged him to tell her all about it.

Herman told his story in his usual straightforward way, though he made as little as possible of what he had suffered.

"Then, mother," he said, "as soon as I found I was not in the right path, I thought I would soon walk into it. I called and I called to father, but no answer came, and I kept hurrying on. Then I was hungry and ate my cake, or at least half of it, for the rest I saved for Bernhard. It is in my pocket now. I did not want it after I got hurt."

"At last it began to grow dark, and I knew then that they had gone home, and that I was left there all alone. It seemed so dismal! I thought if I ever got home again, I would not mind father's not liking me; it seemed such a nice home, with the warm fire, and the supper, and all the faces I loved around the table! But it kept growing darker and colder, and I tried to find some sort of a shelter. I was so tired, mother! When it got to be bedtime, I knew Minna and Bernhard were saying their prayers, and so I thought I would say mine.

So I knelt down and prayed to our dear Lord to take care of me. After that it did not seem so dark and lonesome, but I had to keep walking and jumping, it was so cold. At last, the first thing I knew, I was falling and falling, ever so far, it seemed. And then I was sure my leg was broken, it hurt so.

"By and by I heard father's voice calling 'Herman!'"

"And I was just going to answer, but I remembered that he would be so angry with me for having such a fall, and I knew I couldn't walk home, and I didn't think he could carry me—Oh, mother, I knew I wasn't worth carrying! So I kept still, and pretty soon I heard the sound of his steps going further and further off. Then it seemed darker and more lonesome than ever, and I called *'Fatber!'* with all my might. But he had gone. And after a while I got to thinking that if they should find me and carry me home, the doctor would have to cut off my leg, and then I would be such a plague to father. He never would want a boy with only one leg. So I thought perhaps the dear Lord wouldn't mind that so much, but would let me go to heaven just the same, and I asked Him. But I don't remember what happened next, only I found the hole I had fallen into—for I thought it was a hole—sheltered me from the cold, and I thought God was very good to let me fall into such a nice place. By and by it began to grow light, and that made home seem nearer. But then I found I was lying on such a narrow piece of the rock that, if I had moved the very least bit, I would have rolled off and gone down, down, ever so far, and been dashed to pieces. Don't you remember what a deep place it is, mother?"

Yes, Doris remembered only too well how deep it was.

"It seemed so strange," continued Herman, "that I should have landed on that piece of rock, instead of going all the way down. But it seemed yet stranger that I should have lain so still all night, instead of rolling over and getting killed. It made me think, just for a little while, mother, that our dear Lord did not care if I was a good-for-nothing, and so He made me keep still on purpose.

"Then I heard father calling again; but I could not get courage to answer him, for of all the bad things I ever had done, this was the very worst. To fall down into such a dangerous place, and break my leg! And I couldn't think of any way he could get me out, unless he came down where I was; and that would be dreadful. But, oh, mother, when I heard your voice, I couldn't help crying out, and wanting to see you! And now, only think, I'm getting well, and father seems so kind. Why, when he saw me down in the crevice, he cried! Yes, I saw him! He cried, mother!"

By this time Doris had to run away and cry too. But she soon came back, and made Herman try to get to sleep, since recalling his sufferings thus had excited him painfully.

The next time the schoolteacher called to see Herman, he said to him:

"Has your brother told you what a first-rate scholar he is making?"

"No, Herr Lehrer," replied Herman. "It's just as hard for Bernhard to learn as it is for me."

"That does not matter. You will remember what you learn all the better. If he were my boy, and I could afford it, I would have him, by and by, go to the Latin school."

"And after that?"

"To the University."

"And then?"

"Why, then, he could become a clergyman, or a professor, or a doctor, and make himself useful."

Herman's color went and came.

"I would be a clergyman, then, if I were he!" he cried.

"So as to preach to people about our dear Lord." But after a moment his eager face clouded over. "Father would never send him to the Latin school. He wants us to be carpenters. And we're just as clumsy as we can be!"

The schoolteacher smiled.

"I would like to be a clergyman myself," he said.

"I would like to be just like Pastor Koeffel."

"Ah! yes," cried Herman, "my grandmother is always talking about him. She says he taught her all she knows. She loves him dearly. I saw him once, and he looked so good."

"Yes, he is good. And without goodness, all the Latin schools, and all the universities in the world, would be of little use to him."

After Herr Lehrer had gone, Herman called his grandmother, and told her all they had been talking about.

"Grandmother," he said, "I long to get well and get out again. While I lie here, and can't do anything but think, think—and my thoughts plague me."

"Yes," she said, "it is very tedious to lie still so many weeks. But what sort of thoughts are they that trouble you?"

"I want to tell you, but I can't."

"Do tell me, dear Herman."

"Well, I keep thinking of all the bad things I have done, and the times I have gotten angry, and then I am afraid our dear Lord does not love me. Do you think He does?"

"I know He does," she answered. "And He will help you not to get angry so easily if you will but ask Him."

"When I can go to school, and run about, and am busy at work, I don't have so much time to think about such things."

"Perhaps that is one reason why our dear Lord has made you lie here idle so many weeks. But instead of thinking all of the time how bad you are, it would be better to keep thinking how good He is."

Herman smiled with pleasure, as he always did when he got hold of a new idea. And then his grandmother soothed him by singing good old hymns, such as they used to sing in her younger days, but had left far behind in the distance, with the good old customs, she said. And she told him that he must never forget what a wonderful escape he had had; but often and often ask our dear Lord why He spared his life on that terrible night, since surely it was to do something for Him. And whatever it should turn out to be, she said, it would be beautiful and blessed, because it would be for God and not for man.

After such talks, Herman always folded his hands as soon as He was left alone, and prayed silently that our dear Lord would take him for His own loving child, and teach him to do His will with all his heart; even if it should be, after all, to turn him into a goose-boy.

At last came the joyful day when he could be taken from his bed and placed in a chair, and sit once more at the table with the rest of the family. And then came the awkward attempt to use the crutches his father had made for him.

Nobody laughed at him now for being clumsy,

only he laughed at himself, and was afraid he never would dare to bear his weight upon the weak leg again.

9

One afternoon when there was no school, the children were left to amuse themselves as they chose, and as by this time they had all learned to do whatever Herman pleased, he proposed to play something that would not oblige him to hobble about with his crutches.

"Let's play school," he said. "I will be the teacher and you shall be the scholars."

"Or else we'll play church," said Bernhard, "and you shall preach a sermon."

Herman smiled, and hesitated a moment.

"I'm afraid it would be wrong," he said.

"Oh, we won't play in fun, we'll play in earnest!" said Bernhard. "Oh, come Herman, let's begin."

"I don't look much like it," said Herman. "I ought to have a gown and bands."

"Here's mother's apron," said Minna. "See, Herman, I'll dress you nicely. There, now you really look like the Herr Pastor. But the congregation is very small."

"Never mind," said Herman, and after a minute's thought he chose for his text the words: "Little children, love one another."

If the play had begun as play, it ended in sober earnest. Herman forgot that he was not a real clergyman, and the children forgot it too. They sat and listened to him with wonder, his words sinking into their very hearts and leaving there an ever abiding impression. His mother, passing the door, stopped to look in. She listened with amazement, and went out to the shop to tell Max. Poor Max, who had called his child a good-for-nothing, instinctively took off his cap, as he stood and heard the simple, untaught eloquence that held him, as it did the children, perfectly transfixed. In the midst of his sermon, Herman suddenly caught a glimpse of his father, as he stood in the doorway, and the old habit of fear came over him so he stopped short.

"Go on," said Max, advancing into the room.

"I can't, father," said Herman, blushing. "We

were only playing make-believe church, and I was just making believe to preach to the children."

Max said no more and went back to his work. But Minna and Bernhard talked about Herman's preaching at school the next day, till half the children were curious to hear for themselves such wondrous little sermons. The schoolteacher overheard the talk, too, and the next time he saw Herman, asked him, playfully, to preach to him as well as to the children. Herman was confused and surprised, and hardly knew what answer to make. But when the teacher saw Max, he received the impression that something quite uncommon had occurred, for Max did nothing but shake his head, and call himself a fool and an idiot, and declare that never again in his life would he trust his own senses.

"You should hear that boy!" he cried. "I declare to you that the words flowed out of his mouth as water flows from a fountain. And the words had sense in them, too! And all his life I have called him a good-for-nothing!"

The next holiday afternoon, Bernhard promised neighbor Goschen's Kurt and Lizette that they could have the privilege of coming to play church at their house, for mother had said so, and mother wouldn't say so unless it was right.

Kurt shrugged his shoulders and Lizette tossed her head. Should they really demean themselves to that degree? Should they permit the neighbor's boy Herman, who never said his lessons half so well as they said theirs, to set himself up to preach to them? Pride said, "Don't go." Curiosity said, "Why, yes, go, and see what it is that has turned the heads of those children." So, at last, they decided to drop in for a few minutes, especially if after the preaching they might play at something more amusing.

Bernhard felt rather uneasy at what he had done. He knew that Herman did not like Kurt or Lizette, and thought it very likely he would refuse to preach for their edification. In fact, Herman did, at first, declare that he was sorry they were coming.

"They'll just go to laughing at us," he said, "and I always get angry when people laugh at me."

"You'll have to get over such ways as that," said Minna. "Who ever saw the Herr Pastor get angry?"

"Ah, but I am not the Herr Pastor," said Herman, "and I hate to be laughed at."

"But there won't be anything to laugh at," said Bernhard. "You preach beautifully."

"Do I?" cried Herman, quite astonished. "Then perhaps that is the reason our dear Lord did not let me fall to the bottom of the crevice that night." He became thoughtful almost to sadness, and though he felt happy, longed for some solitary place where he could cry without being seen.

Kurt came in the afternoon adorned with his

most waggish air. He said he and Lizette had made up their minds that it would be nicer to play school than to play church. He wanted to be the teacher, and was sure he would make a vastly better one than the teacher they had now. Herman consented at once but Minna and Bernhard were disappointed. However, books and slates were produced, and Kurt enacted the teacher so well that scarcely one of the children escaped without a shaking or a blow. He found this amusement excellent, till Lizette, getting angry, returned the box on the ear he had just given her with all her strength. He then became furious, and there would have been a serious fight, had not Adolph ran crying to his mother, and told her what was going on. She soon stopped the clash, and, after sitting for a time in sullen silence, Kurt and Lizette condescended to eat an apple or two and peace was finally restored.

"How odd one must feel, hobbling about with crutches!" cried Kurt. "I say, Herman, lend them to me a moment. I want to see how it feels to have your leg broken."

"You can't tell by just using crutches," said Herman. "My leg is now about as good as it ever was, only I am still afraid to bear my full weight on it."

Kurt found moving about with the crutches even more amusing than teaching school, and so spent the rest of the afternoon in frisking around the room with them. When he and Lizette reached home and their mother asked them what sort of preaching they had heard, he replied:

"Pooh! *he* can't preach. He made me keep school and eat apples, and hop around with his crutches all the afternoon. I knew he couldn't preach."

"And even if he could," said Lizette, "I don't suppose he could do it any better than we could. But he just wants to set himself up above us."

"Ah! but if your father were alive, you could hold up your heads as high as they," said Babele.

Before the snow was off the ground, Herman was able to go to school again. Max said no more about making him into a goose-boy, but made a little sled and towed him to school himself, not daring to trust him to the guidance of the other children. The schoolteacher gave him a cordial welcome, and all the boys and girls came out to look at him with great curiosity.

These were the beginning of happy days for Herman. The schoolteacher knew how to encourage him, and at home his father was much changed. It is true that the force of habit made him still often rough and severe, but Herman knew now what a big warm heart lay hidden under the scarlet vest, and that his father really loved him. And we can bear almost anything from those who love us. This is one of God's mercies. Otherwise there would be few happy households, faulty as most human beings are.

Thus things went on through the winter, and spring found Max and his household all in unusual health and spirits. Max had had plenty of work all winter, and in spite of the expense of Herman's illness he had still managed to lay aside as much as usual against the rainy day. Doris had spun quantities of fine linen, and knit an endless number of stockings. The dear old grandmother had also been able to accomplish more than usual. Her health was certainly better since Max left off harassing Doris so perpetually about the children. Little Adolph was now able to go to school with the rest, and for many hours of every day she could sit with her Bible before her, knitting and meditating and reading by turns, and preparing many a future benediction for every one of them, by silent, fervent prayers in their behalf. How many an aged mother fancies herself "in the way," and longs to be gone whose prayers are like guardian angels in the house and home!

10

It was Easter morning, and Doris let all the children sleep a little over the usual time, while she and her mother moved noiselessly about in the garden in a mysterious way. Doris had lost the anxious look she used to wear, and was now a perfect picture of a bright and happy young wife and mother. There was no need to hold up those short skirts of hers as she tripped lightly over the grass still wet with the morning dew; all she had to think of was the basket on her arm and the four children for whom she was preparing a pleasure. The basket was filled with eggs, some pure white, and some red and green and blue. Under every bush, and here and there among the grass, she hid them away; the grandmother did likewise, till all the eggs were gone.

And now it was time to call the children and to remind them that the hens always laid such remarkable Pasch eggs on this auspicious day. Instantly they sprang from their beds, and soon were running eagerly about the garden, gathering in the prizes with laughter and delight.

"How can the hens know it is Easter!" cried little Adolph. "Every year they lay for us such beautiful eggs, but they never laid such lots and lots as they have this time!"

While they were rejoicing over their treasures, they saw the schoolteacher coming up the road with a basket on his arm.

Max, who was leaning on the gate, watching the children, took off his cap, and invited him to come in for breakfast. Though Doris was herself the daughter of a village teacher, the thought of entertaining one at her table threw her into a perfect flurry of pride and pleasure. She ran hither and thither to get the best the house afforded, made pancakes, brought out sauerkraut and boiled eggs. Nothing seemed to her good enough for her guest.

She would have given her right hand for a loaf of white bread to set before him.

After breakfast was over, and the teacher had

spoken a friendly word to each child, he beckoned Max to follow him out to the bench beneath the linden tree.

"Steiner," he said, "I want to ask you what you mean to make of your boys?"

"My father was a carpenter," returned Max, "and so was his father before him, and I expected, till lately, to make my boys follow in the old track."

"But you have changed your mind?"

"Why, no, not exactly. But since you put it into my head that my boys were not, after all, dull, as we used to think them; and since I've heard my Herman get up and preach off a regular sermon, all out of his own head, I've been thinking whether somebody else couldn't make more out of them than I could. They don't take to the trade, either of them."

"Could you afford to send them to the Latin school?"

Max rubbed his head and tried to think what to say. Could he take all those beloved, hard earned savings of his, and see them spent before his face and eyes?

"You can't suppose I'm a rich man," he at last answered evasively. "I won't deny that I've a little laid by against a rainy day, but it would cost a great deal to undertake to make two scholars out of one house."

"That is true," replied the other, "but I think it

my duty to tell you that these boys are very remarkable in many ways. As carpenters they may
make a living, and lead comparatively useful and
happy lives. But our dear Lord has seen fit to
make them more fit for different work."

Max moved uneasily in his seat, as he was accustomed to do when troubled.

"We never had a scholar in our family," he said.
"I don't know as I care to have my boys brought
up to despise their forefathers. It seems to me
that the trade that was good enough for me is
good enough for them."

"But you say they are unusually awkward at the
business."

"Yes, but they are slow at their books, too," returned Max.

"Slow and sure," said the schoolteacher. "Both
the boys have peculiar minds, I will admit;
Herman especially. But I do not think you would
regret giving them an education if you can afford it."

"I will think it over, Herr Lehrer," said Max.

"Pshaw!" he said to himself when the schoolteacher had taken leave, "how would he know
what a pair of boys will turn out to be? Have I
not always known they were dull at their books?
And am I to spend all I have laid up for my old
age in having their heads filled with Latin and
such trash? I was never taught Latin, and see now,
I have a house of my own, a bit of land, cows,

hens, geese, and money laid up into the bargain. To be sure, it would be a great thing to see my Herman in gown and bands, and to hear people saying: 'That is Max's Herman!' But then the money! All my little savings that it has taken me years to rake and scrape together! No, a carpenter I am, and carpenters I will have for my sons. Ha! it would be a pretty thing to have a pair of wiseacres in the house, continually setting their mother and me right!"

In this mood he dressed himself in his holiday suit, and went with all his household to church. The dream of Doris' had so far come true, that Max had silver buttons in his vest and silver buckles at his knees. He looked handsome in her eyes, as now and then she glanced at him across the church. There seemed to be something in his face today that had thus far been missing there. This was really the case. New thoughts and new feelings had been awakened in his mind, and a mighty struggle was going on within, between love and pride on the one hand, and avarice and the force of habit on the other.

"Doris," he said, as they walked home together, "if we choose, we may one day see our Herman stand and preach like the Herr Pastor today. Only I would have it understood that he would never preach sermons one could not comprehend."

"The Herr Pfarrer is a very learned man," replied Doris. "Very likely he himself understands all that he says, which must make the preaching agreeable to him, though dull to us. But what were you saying about our Herman?"

Max repeated to her all the schoolteacher had said.

In the first flush of her surprise and pleasure Doris said some foolish things, which she afterward wished she had not said.

"I knew it would puff you up," said Max.

"Well, and no wonder," cried Doris, "if after the way people have behaved about our boys! And I knew all along that they were not of the common sort. You should hear Babele Goschen run on about her children."

"If Herr Pastor was not so high and mighty, one might ask his advice," said Max.

"Yes, if he were but like our blessed Pastor Koeffel. Max, why don't you go and consult with him? Think now—he baptized us both, when we were little, and surely he would take an interest in our affairs now."

"But the money, Doris! The money!"

"What is money good for unless it is used?" she returned. "Oh, Max! we will work day and night, and do without this and that, but we will make scholars of our boys. Ah! I always said they were not dull. I knew it in my heart of hearts."

"Nay," said Max, "but you must remember that we shall be old one of these days and not able to work by day, much less by night. I may lose my health and be disabled, and then what would become of us? Think, now, all we have saved and laid by with so much care must go to those two boys. And there are Minna and Adolph to consider."

"Your mother has often said she would leave all she had to Minna. And as for Adolph, never fear for him. He can turn his hand to anything."

"But all my life's savings!" said Max. "Everything going out and nothing coming in. Other boys will be earning and saving, and taking wives and settling down, while ours are eating—no, studying, I mean—their heads off. And in our old age we shall be beggars, Doris."

Doris would not be convinced. She could not imagine Max as ever growing old. There was his mother, now, as erect and blooming as a young maiden, and doing more hard work in the open air than many men. And at any rate the dear Lord had made the boys just as they were, and it was plainly His will that they should make uncommon men. Had not they always abhorred and shunned rude and bad boys? Had not Herman made himself unpopular in the village by shrinking from all the wild games they played?

"I will go and consult with my mother," said Max at length. "Herman can go with me tomorrow when there will be no school. People say she has more than silver pennies laid aside. Who knows what she may choose to do with them?"

11

Accordingly they set off early next morning, and as they walked cheerfully along, Max was struck with the intelligent questions asked by Herman. He wondered how he had not observed before what a thoughtful boy he was, and felt ashamed of the rough answers he had often made to just such questions.

As they approached the village where his mother lived, Max felt very much as if he had brought some strange and rare animal for her inspection. She had always held Herman in supreme contempt. His sensibility outraged her undemonstrative nature, and she never could forgive him for being so much like his mother in character. Not that she had anything to say against Doris, not she. She thanked Heaven she knew better than to find fault with her sons' wives. But Max might have married a rich wife had he chosen, and would any body go so far as to pretend that Doris was rich?

As for Herman, he stood in mortal terror of his "big grandmother," as he mentally called her, to distinguish her from the "little grandmother" at home. He always appeared his very worst in her presence, was sure to spill his coffee on her table, and to upset her stocking basket, and tangle her yarn around his unlucky legs.

"Well, Max," she said, without stopping her spinning wheel, "so you've come at last."

"Yes, mother, and here is our Herman, come also. You have not seen him since his accident in the winter."

Herman took off his cap and made his best bow.

"A pretty little sum he has cost you!" said the big grandmother, eyeing the boy from head to foot.

"Yes, but that is now over," said Max, rubbing his hands. "Go out, Herman, and amuse your-self. I have some important things to speak of."

"Aye, and so have I," said the mother, as

Herman withdrew. "I have bought the forty acre lot, and taken a man to work it."

"The forty acre lot!" repeated Max slowly.

"Yes, that I have. And it brings me in a penny or two—trust me for that. And if you do not believe me, you can take a look into my stable and see what I have there."

"Yes, I have no doubt of it," said Max absently. "But, mother, I want to consult you about Herman."

"Very likely. But do you know that I have four horses in my stable, besides six oxen and seven cows?"

"Yes, yes, it is truly wonderful," said Max. "When I think about how my poor father left things! But, mother, about my Herman?"

"You want me to take him as my cow-boy, at last? Nay, then, but you are too late. I hired one exactly one week ago today."

"Hang her cow-boy and her four horses, and her cattle!" said Max irreverently to himself. "We have found out that our Herman is a most wonderful boy!" he said to her.

"Humph!" said the mother, and began to spin again.

"And we are thinking of making a scholar of him."

"Humph!"

"His teacher thinks we ought," said Max desperately. "Do advise me, mother."

"Then I advise you to take this bit of wool, which I present you as a freewill offering, and fill both ears with it. The boy is dull, I tell you. I saw it from the outset. A scholar, indeed!"

"I shall do what I like with him!" cried Max.

"Of course. And do what you like with your Minna, for not a penny of mine shall she touch if you waste your savings on that silly boy."

"You shall not call him silly twice to my face," cried Max. "Come here, Herman," he called from the door.

Herman came in panting, and seeing the passion his father was in, hesitated on the threshold.

"Come in, child," said Max, "and stand upon this chair, and let your grandmother hear you preach."

Herman shrank into half his size.

"Oh, father! Don't make me! I can't! I don't know what to say."

"Say what you said before," said Max, taking him by the arm and making him mount into a chair.

Poor Herman stood in the chair, a piteous sight.

"I don't remember what I said before. Oh, father, please let me get down!"

"Say something new then. Come on, I will have your grandmother hear you."

"I can't think of anything. It came of itself before. Oh, dear father, please let me get down!"

His father's displeasure and disappointment and his grandmother's cold scorn were more than he could bear. He covered his face with his hands and burst into tears.

"Then get down and be off with you," said the grandmother. "You have taken all the polish from my chair as usual."

Herman flew from the room and from the house. He would have been glad to fly from the world.

"I see there's no use in trying to convince you, mother," said Max. "The child was frightened, and no wonder. But I must do him justice whether you will or not. And I say you will hear from him one of these days, when he will perhaps interest you as much as your new man and your horses and your cattle do now."

Then regretting that he had thus spoken, for after all was she not his mother?, he said:

"I hope your man is faithful and industrious?"

"You may well hope so," she answered.

"And treats you with respect?"

"Let me alone for that, thank heaven."

"Who is he? One of the men from the village?"

"His name is Peter Fuchse."

"Peter Fuchse! What, he is your hired man? You are joking, mother."

"Nay, I did not say I hired him. I married him yesterday," she replied.

Max started to his feet.

"It is time for me to be gone," he cried. "Peter Fuchse! My father's old enemy! Oh, mother! May God forgive you, but this is a cruel, wicked shame!"

He took his cap and turned to go. Once he looked sorrowfully back, hoping to see some sign of tenderness, one look of regret on her large, cold face. He went out into the fresh air, hardly knowing which way to take. For the moment, darkness seemed to have fallen on the face of the whole earth, and everything real to have left it forever. He called Herman, and took him by the hand in token of forgiveness, and walked home-ward with rapid strides.

"After this you have but one grandmother," he said at last to Herman.

"Which one is it?" asked Herman. "The little one?"

"Yes, the little one."

As they stepped inside the door, and Doris came joyfully to meet them, Max stretched out his arms and held her to his breast, for he knew now all she was to him.

"You are all I have left now," he said.

"What hashappened, dear Max? Your mother—"

"Has married Peter Fuchse! Peter Fuchse with his horses, his cattle, and his cows. Peter Fuchse who drove my father into his grave! Oh, Doris!"

Doris was too shocked to speak. She cried over him a little, and then ran to get the best supper she could think of. Once she stopped to kiss her mother, and to say half laughing, half in earnest:

"Think, mother? it might have been you!"

Max ate his supper, which was none the less agreeable that his mother had not offered him a dinner, and was comforted. That Herman should go to the Latin school was now a settled thing. His mother's opposition had done more to move him than the urgency of Doris.

"If it costs me my last penny, and I have to sell the roof from over our heads, my boys shall be put into positions where their grandmother shall have to look up to them in spite of herself."

"Dear Max," said Doris' mother, laying her hand gently on his shoulder, "don't talk thus. If you educate the boys, let it be so that they may be more useful, and because our dear Lord seems to choose to have it so."

Max looked up at her kindly.

"We'll do it for all sorts of reasons," he said "yours, and mine, and the dear mother's."

12

It was not time for Herman to leave the village school yet, but it was thought best to tell him that he was not to be made a carpenter, but to go to the Latin school in the next village, and learn a great many things that boys were not usually taught.

"And is Bernhard to go, too?" asked Herman. "Because the schoolteacher said Bernhard was such a good scholar, and he did not say I was."

"We shall see," replied Max.

Not a little talk went on in the village when it

became known what Max meant to do with his boy Herman. Babele Goschen especially, as their particular friend and neighbor, felt called upon to bear the whole burden of the boy's schooling, which she said would cost all the money Max could make for years to come. And why was Herman, she would like to know, to be set up above other boys and have it put into his head that he should aim to be a clergyman?

Max, however, did not disturb himself about what people said, but worked on with patient industry, saying little about his plans or his boys, and every week laying aside something toward the future. His shame and sorrow about his mother was toning down the harshness of his character. He saw, too, to what lengths the love of money might carry one, since it had led her to form this disgraceful marriage, and had hardened her heart against her very own children. Thus the sacrifice he was making in behalf of Herman had its ennobling effect, and was elevating him above himself. Then began to arise in his soul occasional misgivings concerning the worldly life he was leading. The noiseless influence of his wife's mother was gradually doing its unconscious work.

A holiday drew Kurt and Lizette to the house one afternoon, and of their own accord they proposed to the children to play at church, and have some preaching.

"Well, so we will," said Herman. He threw his mother's red apron over the back of a chair and placed himself on a block of wood behind it. Minna found another apron to serve as a gown. Herman had cut wood on this block for many a year. It served very well, however, as pulpit, and Adolph rang the bell for church, as soon as everything was arranged.

Minna came to her seat with her doll in her arms, when everybody cried that playthings were not allowed in church.

"But mothers take their babies," urged Minna, "and mine never cries."

The sermon began. At first with some hesitation and shyness, but after a few moments Herman forgot everything in his subject, and a torrent of words came pouring out that would have astonished even himself if he would have stopped to think of himself. He uttered a child's thoughts in a child's language, but with such vivacity and earnestness that every word went to the heart. Minna's head sank lower and lower as he went on. Her doll lay forgotten upon her lap, as something within her seemed to whisper: "You have always been called a good child, and no one has found fault with you as they have with Herman, and yet he loves our dear Lord better than you do." For Herman spoke from his own experience. He had been misunderstood, and solitary, and was almost brokenhearted. He had suffered bodily pain and mental anguish. He had prayed to God, and God had heard him, and now he would have all these children pray too.

Bernhard, lost in admiration, sat spellbound in his chair. He forgot that sore subject, the short sleeves of his jacket, about which he had been accustomed to cry, and to wish his arms would not grow so fast. He saw and heard nothing but Herman, and his eager face and glowing words.

It was curious to watch the faces of Kurt and Lizette. They were determined not to be serious, and not to admire, yet in spite of themselves they listened with wonder, almost with disbelief.

"He gets it all out of some book," Lizette whispered. "But he says it all so beautifully. It seems as if he really was in earnest, but he's only making believe."

But now the sermon was ended, and Herman jumped down from his block, flushed and excited. "Good-bye," said Kurt, "we must go now. I shouldn't wonder if after you'd been to the Latin school you could say something out of your own head."

He returned home with Lizette in silence, and with unconscious envy in his heart.

Meanwhile another little audience had listened to the sermon, father and mother and grandmother, with beating hearts and fingers on their lips. As the congregation within broke up, they retreated from the door where they had been listening, and the children came quietly out of the room.

"It's perfectly wonderful," said Max. "There never was anything like it in my family. If that boy is dull and stupid, I would like to see one who isn't, that's all."

"It is very plain what he was meant for," said Doris, wiping some tears of pride and pleasure from her eyes. "Mother, you must tell him. All the good things he knows you have taught him."

That night, after Herman was in bed, his grandmother went to him.

"You see now that our dear Lord knew all the time what you were good for."

"Am I really good for anything?" cried Herman, starting up.

"Of course you are. You are good at preaching."

"Oh! that's nothing. I just say the words, that's all."

"But when you are a man, it will be different. Think, now, your dear father is going to spend on you all he had saved for his old age. One of these days you will be a learned man, and if you are good, as well as learned, perhaps you will be a real clergyman, and can teach the people to love God. But the main thing will be to love Him yourself. Without that, all the learning in the world would be of no use."

"Oh! I never shall be good enough to be a

clergyman, grandmother. Think what a temper I've got!"

"Yes, I know. But you must conquer that."

Herman shook his head, yet pleasant thoughts were in it, and he fell asleep and had yet pleasanter dreams.

Meanwhile Kurt and Lizette talked not a little, at school, about Herman and his performances, and before long he was called, "Herr Pastor," and "The Little Preacher," all over the village.

At first he shrank from these titles, given as they were in derision, but after a time they ceased annoying him under the pressure of new interests. For Max was resolved to delay no longer placing him in the Latin school, which, being in the next village, he could attend every day while coming home at night.

For a few weeks Herman suffered agonies of shyness in his new sphere. His teachers would have misjudged and overlooked him, had not rumors from his own village reached them, which prepared them to do him justice. His new schoolmates were inclined to laugh at him and his clothes, and all he did and said. This led to some flashes of the Steiner temper, and many tears of repentance on his part. Every night, when he went home, he had his day's experience to relate. His grandmother watched him with anxiety, knowing to what varied temptations he was now exposed. But as for Max and Doris, they were

too proud of him to doubt that he would turn
out well.

The most trying thing he had to contend with
was the frequent meetings with his "big grandmother," the Latin school being in her village.

Seeing him shrink from her in terror, she took
pains to thrown herself in his way, and found it
very amusing to see the color come and go in his
cheek at her rough salutations. She tortured him
to such a degree that oftentimes he was tempted
to beg his father to let him leave school alto-
gether, but real love of knowledge held him back.
These encounters with her, and with the boys
who took delight in teasing him, made the getting home at night very pleasant. There was such
a welcome awaiting him from everyone, and the
old smoke-stained room looked so pleasant!

Thus a year passed away when things began to
take another turn. Max, who had never had a
pain, or known a day's illness, one day caught a
violent cold, neglected it, and was seized with a
fever. Week after week passed and he lay helpless
upon his bed, broken in body and broken in
spirit, and suffering fearfully with pain. At first
he would have Herman keep on with his school,
but gradually they had to consent to his staying
at home. There were cattle to attend to, and cows,
and Doris had more than she could do to take
care of Max, while her mother, with Minna's
help, did the rest. Herman had not forgotten, and

never could forget, what his father had done for him during his own illness, and he now devoted his every spare moment to his comfort. During the year he had grown up tall without losing his strength. He could therefore help lift his father, and in many other ways make himself useful.

As Max became more and more feeble, he began to look at Herman with wistful eyes, as if there was something he wanted to say to him that he had not strength to say. Everyone observed it, but no one dared ask what it meant. One day, however, when Herman was alone with his father, this yearning look went so to his heart that he was constrained to speak.

"Dear father," he said, "you want to say something to me, and cannot. If it is about my education, don't give it another thought. While you are so sick, I could not study, if I would, and if you never get well, I will take your place, and learn to be a carpenter, and mother and the children shall not suffer want."

An expression of infinite relief spread itself over the face of Max, and for a time he seemed to have done with care, and to have nothing to do but to get well. But it was not long before his face assumed a yet more anxious expression, amounting, at times, to horror, so that Doris and the children shrank from seeing him.

The words of Herman, "If you should not get well," had suggested the question whether he was fit to die, and in his enfeebled state he could ill afford to grapple with such a question. In his days of health he had not troubled himself with such questions. He said to himself that he did about as well as he knew how, and far better than some of his neighbors, that he had never defrauded any man, and that God was merciful. And, at all events, there would be plenty of time to attend to his soul when sickness or old age would lay him aside from work that now occupied every moment. And now he had, indeed, plenty of time—but what sort of time? He could not fix his mind on any subject two minutes together. There was only a vague sense of misery and fearful uncertainty.

In the midst of this illness, there came a message from his mother that Peter Fuchse had been kicked by one of the horses and lay at the point of death. They did not trouble him with this news, but returned the answer that Max lay, likewise, in a critical state.

Thus week after week dragged slowly on, and then there came a slight change for the better. The pain subsided, and Max lay, day after day, night after night, in profound sleep. They were obliged to awaken him to give him nourishment and restoratives, otherwise he would have slept away his life. His care was now less painful to his friends, but not less serious. He needed more tender, judicious nursing than the tiniest infant.

And while he lay thus, hovering between life and death, another little daughter was born, and as Doris pressed her to her heart, her faith in God was weak, and her anguish strong within her, as she asked why the one must be given and the other taken away.

"Don't ask why, dear," her mother said, "we never can be happy till we stop asking why."

"I don't want to be happy," said Doris. "To think that I am lying here, idle, when my Max needs me so much!"

"The Herr Lehrer sat with him last night, and even you, Doris, could not be more tender and kind. Herman slept well, and tonight he will be able to sit up again. Dear child, can't you trust Max to our Lord?"

"No, mother, I cannot. The doctor says everything depends on nursing now, and, oh, with all there is to think of, some of you will forget to waken him at the right moment. And I can't live without Max! do you hear, mother? I can't live without him!"

"You cannot put yourself in the place of God, my Doris. You may watch day and night and do everything the doctor directs, but only our dear Lord can make what you do to prosper. Try, dear, not to have any will of your own. Try, dear. I am an old woman, and have had my sorrows, and have done fighting against my Lord."

Doris looked at her mother, as she spoke these

words in her gentle, tender way, which yet was so full of conviction, and was struck with the heavenly expression of her countenance. She hid her face in the pillow, and in broken fragments of prayer tried to say, "Not my will, but Thine, Oh, God." But how hard it was to say it with faith and holy courage! She was afraid, even while the words were on her lips, that He would take her at her word, and snatch away everything she loved better than she loved Himself.

"Mother," she said at last, "how came you to feel so differently from what I do? Did it come all of itself? When you were as young as I am now, hadn't you a will of your own?"

"Indeed I had, my Doris. And idols of my own as well. But our dear Lord took pains with me, and bore with me, and kept on teaching me as fast as I kept on forgetting. And when He found nothing else would do, He used the rod—ah, yes! He used the rod. First of all, He took away my little Herman. He was a brave boy and I was proud of him, and so he had to go. Then I ran straight to my dear Lord, just as little Adolph runs to you when you chastise him, for I was very sorry, and thanked Him for afflicting me."

"*Thanked* Him! Oh, no, mother!"

"Nay, but what would you have of your child, my Doris? So then, seeing how sorrowful I was, and how I really did want to love Him more than all else besides—He took my Kilian, my little heart's child, the very one I could least spare. And then—Oh, my Doris! you know it all—one child after another came and went. It seemed as if all they came for was to tear me in pieces in the going! And then, last of all, hardest of all, I had to let go of my hold on your dear father, and let him go, too."

"But mother, while God was doing such dreadful things to you did you keep on loving Him?"

"Keep on! Why, don't you see, my Doris, that they made me love Him more than ever? For these were the answers to my prayers."

"Yes, I see. But He does not take such dreadful ways to answer everybody's prayers."

"He takes the very best way, my Doris."

"But, mother, think how many people never have any trouble. They never lose their children, and everything goes on smoothly. Why should they have such nice times, and you have such hard times? I don't understand."

Her mother only smiled. But finally she said: "I do not know, and I do not want to know, at least not now. And then as to the nice times! Ah! God gives them to those who love Him!"

"Mother, you are such a wonderful woman."

"No, dear. But we have a wonderful Savior."

Doris said no more. She only clasped her hands, and looked upward.

At that moment Herman came softly walking into the room.

"Dear father is awake," he said, "and knows us all. He keeps asking for you, mother."

"In three days I shall be up and about," cried Doris eagerly. "Go, Herman, and tell him so. Or stay, take the baby to him, that he may know why I forsake him."

"No, dear," said her mother, "but we will tell him you will soon be there."

But the little one, resenting the style in which she was overlooked, set up a shrill cry that announced to her father that there was a new voice in the house.

He smiled as he heard it.

"Bring the little thing to me," he said.

But when they brought it, his eyes filled with tears, and he said: "I am just as helpless as that feeble baby."

Yet he grew strong faster than the baby did, and was soon able to sit up in bed and act like himself. And yet unlike himself, for his long illness had taught him lessons that were to renovate his life.

"I shall be a better husband after this," he said to Doris, at their first joyful meeting.

"And I shall be a better wife," she answered.

"I don't see how that can well be. But, as for myself, I have thought too much about this world, and too little about the next."

"So have I," said Doris.

"But when I came to face death, I saw what a

mistake I had been making all my life long. Ah! Doris, it is a great thing to die!"

"Yes," she answered, "and so it is to live and get ready to die."

After a pause, she added:

"Something very serious happened while you were sick. Peter Fuchse was kicked by one of his horses and is dead."

"It may be the saving of my mother," said Max. "Give me the baby. What a tender, soft little thing she is! Do you know, dear old Doris, what I want to call this child?"

Doris changed color. Was Max going to give the little one his mother's name, now that she was left so rich?

Max saw what she was fearing.

"You need not be afraid of that," he said. "No, I am going to give my child the name of the best woman in the world. She shall have your mother's name, and be called Magdalena."

This was a happy moment for Doris, but she could not speak a word.

"You see, my mother could give silver florins, but your mother will give prayers," said Max.

And now came the question of how their affairs were standing. Herman brought the account book, and showed his father what had been spent during his illness, and what was yet to be paid. There was enough to pay off every debt and to keep them all comfortable until Max could fully recover. But that was all. Herman must not go back to school.

"Don't look so distressed father," he said, at the close of this discussion. "I have known it all along. And I am not so awkward and clumsy as I used to be. You shall see a bookcase I have made for the Herr Lehrer, while you were sick. I am sure I can make a carpenter, and help you to support the family. And perhaps, by and by, we can send Bernhard to school, if I give up going."

All the prayers and tears that enabled Herman thus cheerfully to renounce the life that had looked so attractive to him, were sacred matters between himself and his God.

Max returned to his shop, and Herman worked faithfully all day long at his trade.

Babele Goschen was relieved thereby of a great care.

"I always said they were throwing away their money," she declared, "and now they've found out that their Herman was no such wonder after all. Folks say he found the lessons too hard, and was glad to settle down to work like other folks. It's hard for them, having the old grandmother to feed. What old folks are for, I can't imagine. Why don't they die off instead of the young ones?"

The first day Max was able to go to his work, he called his household together, and read a chapter from the large Bible, and prayed.

"I came up, as it were, from death," he said, "and it is fitting that I should begin a new life."

And this came about from having "that old grandmother to feed."

13

Max was not so strong since his illness as he was before and could not do so much in a day. He could not help feeling troubled that all he made must be spent. The old habit of pinching and saving had still much power over him. It was necessary for Doris to take a maid to help her in the household tasks, for she was never herself after the anxiety and fatigue of Max's sickness. And there was this obstacle in the way of her recovering her strength—the baby gave her no rest, day or night, but was a marvel of wakefulness, a regular watchdog, her father called her, enough to frighten away all the robbers in the world.

Some of the old women said she was crying for something which, if she could once have, she would forever after hold her peace. Various extraordinary articles of food were accordingly administered, but none of them proving to be the right one, the baby kept on crying, and Doris kept on walking the room with her, in order, if possible, to let Max sleep quietly, at least through his first sleep. Naturally enough, as their cares increased, and their health and strength decreased, both Max and Doris grew less lively and talkative. The neighbors said they were growing old, and some said they were getting too religious.

Meanwhile there was no communication between Max and his mother. He had not time or strength to go to see her, and she could not take one of her six horses from the field long enough to go to him. She drove all before her, bought more land and more cattle, and, the neighbors declared, grew younger and more blooming every day. Peter Fuchse had left her houses and land and cattle, his own vile name, and a character much degenerated by his influence.

Every remembrance of her brought pain to Max. He felt that it was owing to her precepts and examples that he had grown up so avaricious and eager for gain. Then all his harshness to his children, was not that in imitation of the treatment he had received from her all his life? Still, she was his mother, and had nourished and brought him up. Yet he had parted from her in anger, and with bitter hatred in his heart.

"I can't stand it this way much longer," he said to Doris. "I must go to see my mother, and try to see if there can be peace between us."

"I fear she will never forgive us the baby's name," said Doris. "Dear Max, is it well to go?"

"Yes, it is well. And the sooner it is over the better. Tomorrow, being a holiday, I will go and have done with it."

The next morning he put on his Sunday suit, and set forth alone. He still looked pale, and his garments hung loosely upon his wasted frame, and when he finally reached his mother's house, he was thoroughly exhausted by the long walk.

Everything looked as it did when, three years ago, he made what he then meant would be his final visit. His mother, not a day older, sat erect as ever at her wheel, and scolded her maids as a pastime.

"Well," she said, exactly as before, "so you've come at last."

"Yes, mother, I have come. You know I have been sick, and could not come sooner."

She just gave him a glance and went on with her spinning. Yet in that brief glance she saw the pale face, the wasted figure, and the loosely fitting garments.

"Hedwig!" she cried through the open doorway, "Hedwig, do you mean to spend the whole day in watering that linen? And you, Martha, can you find nothing better to do with your hands than to roll them in your apron?"

The frightened maids took speedy flight in confusion.

"They say the storks have brought your Doris another daughter," she continued in the same tone.

"Yes," said Max.

"And you have doubtless given it my name, now that I am become rich," she cried with a boisterous laugh.

"No, I have not given it your name, mother," he answered quietly. I call it Magdalena, for its grandmother."

"Ah! she has so much to give it for its dowry!"

"I will tell you the honest truth, mother. My long sickness has made me another man."

"So I see."

"Nay, but listen, mother. I mean that it has put new thoughts into my mind. It has shown me that there are things of more value than houses and lands."

He waited a moment, but there was no comment, only the wheel flew faster than ever.

"I used to put them first," he added at last, "but now I put first eternal salvation for me and my house."

"Have you anything more to say?" she asked,

and joined a broken thread with infinite care.

"Nothing, mother. Only as you are getting old, and sickness and death must come sooner or later—"

"Getting old?" she cried. "Ha, ha! I never was so young in my life. But now it is my turn to speak. What have you done with that boy Herman?"

"He is at home, and works at his trade."

"Works at his trade, does he? How dare you look me in the face, Max Steiner? You think, I suppose, that I have neither eyes nor ears. Let me tell you, then, that I know quite well what they say of him in the Latin school, and what they think of you for taking him out of it. His trade, indeed! When, with such wits as his, he might one day become Staats-Minister."

"You do not understand the case, mother. In the first place, my sickness made it necessary to take him from school. In the second place, the idea of making a great man of him has never crossed my mind."

"It has crossed mine, though," she answered sharply.

"At any rate, I can't help it that I am not the man I was; and that I have not now the money necessary to educate Herman."

"And I suppose I have not either," she said, and round flew the wheel.

"You don't mean, mother—"

"Yes, I do mean. The fact is, I always knew that all that ailed your Herman was having too much sense. He inherited it from me. Oh, you needn't smile. I know all about it, child. Do you suppose that if I hadn't more sense than most folks, I would be the richest woman in the village? People may call it luck if they choose, but I say it isn't luck. It's sense. And if I had been a boy instead of a girl, and been sent to school instead of to work in the field, I would be one of your learned men at this minute. Thank heaven, red hair and a fiery temper ain't the only things Herman has gotten from me. He'll make us all proud of our name, mark my words."

"But mother—"

"Nay, let me talk now. The boys may come, I say, there is room enough in this house that I have rebuilt," she added, looking grandly about her. "The Latin school is but a stone's throw hence, and as for the money, you may thank Peter Fuchse that he has left me a few florins, ha! ha!"

At the name of Peter Fuchse, Max reddened and then grew pale.

I cannot have my boys indebted to that man, he cried.

"Pshaw! Well, then, I have a few florins of my own it is just possible. And as I was saying, the boys may come, but they may not go. I shall henceforth resume the name of Steiner, and the boys shall bring honor to it. After all, Peter was a bad, vile man. I am not sorry to forget him. Yes, let the boys come and divert my mind."

"But mother—"

"Nay, it is all settled. Latin school, university, books, clothes, I shall pay for all out of my own pocket. And as to the clothes, let me tell you that your Doris will not know her own sons when she sees them. I shall not sentence them to go with eight or ten inches of bare wrist grown beyond their jacket sleeves as she does."

"You forget, mother, that we have been forced to be saving. Besides, have not you boxed my ears more than once, for making a fuss about just such jackets?"

"Well, let it pass. Let it pass. Ah, there is one thing I came near forgetting to say. The boys are to leave behind them all the sanctimonious, solemn ways your Doris and her mother have taught them. I won't have such things in my house. I want nothing around me but what is cheerful and pleasant."

"But my boys are like two young birds," said Max. "Why, mother, do you really imagine that religion makes them gloomy?"

"No, I don't fancy. I know it. Young birds indeed! Why, your Herman, whenever I met him, when he was here at the school, was like a solemn little owl."

"That is because he is so afraid of you mother. And he is really a God-fearing boy."

"He must be cured of that. He has sense enough to make his way in the world if one drives that nonsense out of him."

"Mother!" his voice made her stop spinning and look at him in dumb amazement. "Mother, my boys shall never come to you on such terms. Sooner than trust them to your hands, I would saw the boards and choose the nails for their coffins: aye, and do it with tears of joy."

"Very well. Have it as you like."

"But can nothing be said, can nothing be done to save you? Not for the sake of the boys, but for your own sake, mother, mark what I say. Life at best is short."

"There, no more, no more. The thing is settled. Go your ways and I will go mine. No child of mine shall ever preach to me or set himself up above me. My mind is made up, and you know, Max Steiner, that you might as well try to move all the mountains in the land as to move me."

Max did know it. He took his cap, cast upon her a look of unspeakable sorrow, and went out. His step as he crossed the threshold was the weary step of an old man. She saw and heard it, and went on spinning.

He crossed the fields, and scarcely looking upon them, yet felt how rich they were. He saw the barns which the men were filling with hay and with grain, and passed them also, as if he saw them not. He was aiming for a grove where in his boyhood he had often fled from his mother's harsh words, to gnash his teeth, and vent the passions and hatred he dared not show. Here he now threw himself upon his knees, and prayed. For he wanted to be sure that he had done right in throwing away what she had offered his boys, and he wanted to quiet the commotion of his spirit.

14

"The dear father is late tonight," said Doris. "His mother has doubtless made him stay to rest himself. It is a pity he did not decide to spend the night with her, and so escape your cries, my little Lena. Adolph, run out and see if your father is in sight."

"Yes, mother, here he comes," said Adolph, "and he looks dreadfully tired."

"I'm getting old, my Doris," he said, smiling as he caught her anxious look.

"I'll have supper directly," she said.

As they gathered about the table, Max patted Adolph's head.

"Father," said the child, "I like you almost as well as mother. You are a great deal nicer than you used to be."

Doris tried to hush him, but Max looked upon him kindly, and said:

"That is true, my little man."

It was a tiresome evening for Doris. Max lay asleep on the bench till bedtime, and she could not ask what sort of a visit he had had. Then when he awoke, and the other children had gone to bed, the baby woke also and began to cry.

"I can't talk when the child is crying," said Max. "Besides, I am too tired to talk. Let us go to sleep now."

"It is easy to say 'Let's go to sleep'," thought Doris, "but it is not so easily done when one has a screaming baby in one's arms. Well, if there was anything good to tell, Max could not keep it to himself, I am sure. I did hope his mother's hard heart would melt when she saw how he looked, and that she would even offer to do something for Herman." "Max," she cried, "Let me just ask one thing before you go to sleep. Did your mother give you a dinner?"

"No, I came away."

"But she offered you wine?"

"No. I—"

"What a mean, stingy, wicked thing! I wonder

you did not drop dead on the way!"

"I never can help laughing when you try to get into a passion," said Max, rousing up. "It is so ridiculous. You make believe in such a poor way. I wouldn't try, if I were you. Now, what will you say when I tell you that she offered to take both the boys off our hands and educate them?"

Doris replied by laying down her baby and running to put both her arms around his neck.

"Wait till you hear the rest. I refused her offer."

"You refused? Oh, Max!"

"Yes, I refused. She would only take them on one condition, and that was, that they would live like a pair of heathen. But I really am too tired to speak another word, especially when I have to shout so as to drown that little woman's voice. Tomorrow I'll tell you everything, and you will come in the end to think I did what was best."

Doris said no more, and after a time the baby fell asleep, and she could snatch a few hours' rest before morning.

But Max must then go to his work, and defer enlightening her curiosity.

When he reached the shop, he found Herman already there, whistling merrily, and engaged on a dainty bit of carving.

"Look, father!" he cried, "I am carving. I invented the pattern, and have done all this."

Max took the wood from Herman's hands and

examined it with care and genuine interest.

"It is well done," he said.

This was high praise from his lips, and Herman was satisfied with it.

"I went to see your grandmother yesterday."

"Yes, father."

"And she proposed to take upon herself the whole expense of your education. And of Bernhard's also." Herman turned pale, and the bit of wood fell from his hands.

"It is too good to be true!" he cried.

"But hear the rest. You are to live with her as long as you are in the Latin school, and promise to live without the fear of God."

Herman stooped to pick up his work from the floor. It was broken.

"Do you think I can fasten this together with glue, father?"

Max was annoyed at this evasion of the subject in hand.

"Stick to the subject," he said in somewhat of his old, hasty way.

"Oh, father! It came upon me so suddenly. When you began, I was so glad, and thankful! Not but that I am contented just as I am. For I really am. But I was so surprised that grandmother would think of such a thing. And it seemed as if our dear Lord really did mean that I should have an education. And then came the disappointment."

"The disappointment?" said Max. "Do you

mean to say that you will not accept your grandmother's offer?"

"All her horses could not drag me there!" replied Herman.

"Thank God!" said Max.

"What did you tell my grandmother, dear father?"

"Pretty much what you have told me," replied Max, smiling.

Herman went on with his work, but there was no more whistling that day. Max looked at him now and then with pride and pleasure.

That night little Lena thought it best to steep and give her parents time to discuss family affairs. Max then gave to Doris the whole history of his visit to his mother.

"But Herman could not have been injured by living with his grandmother," said Doris, "he is so decided and steady. And think of the good he might have done to her!"

"I knew how you would feel," said Max. "But if you should ever have to stand face to face with death, as I have done, you would see as plainly as I do, that I have chosen well for my boys. And I am thankful to say that Herman is satisfied with my choice."

Doris sighed.

"What will Babele Goschen say, I wonder?" she thought. "Well, I dare say, dear Max is right. But such a chance will never come again."

It was some relief, when she talked it over with her mother, to find that she quite justified Max.

"But Herman is growing up so tall and straight, and to see him standing in the pulpit, with gown and bands like our Herr Pastor, would be a sight, indeed."

"Yet since our dear Lord will not have it so, we must not fret about it," said the grandmother. "The time has been that we were satisfied to have the boys become carpenters, and surely they might be in a worse business."

"Yes, there is Babele's boy Kurt beginning to idle away his time at the alehouse," said Doris. "I am ashamed to think how ungrateful I am."

The little household now settled down for the winter in peace. Minna had gotten through the usual round of studies at the village school, and was now at home, ready to help her mother in all the household cares and labors. She always had been a sober and quaint little damsel, and now she became everybody's right hand. She made the bread, and boiled the soup, and swept the house. On Sundays she laid out upon their beds the holiday suits and the clean linen for her father and brothers, and at night her careful hands restored everything to its place again. The maid could now find leisure to help with the spinning, and another cow was bought so that butter might be made for the market. In all the village there was not so well ordered or so happy a household.

Since Herman had developed a taste for carving, Max allowed him to devote himself to it, as a business, and it proved to be both profitable and pleasurable. The long winter evenings were given him for his own use, and, as well as he could, he kept on with his studies for the mere love of them. The Herr Lehrer came occasionally to give him a little help, but it was not much he could give, for, though himself richly endowed by nature, he was poor, and his education was limited. He had a wife and a child and little leisure for study.

15

"Dear mother," said Doris, as she sat in the midst of her family one wintry night, "how happy and contented we all are! I am glad now that Herman lives at home with us, instead of being off in the world, worrying over books and forgetting his old home. But after I heard the beautiful sermons he preached to the children, I truly thought he was cut out for a preacher."

"They still call me the 'little clergyman,' in the village," said Herman, looking up with a smile. "And I am nearly as tall as father! But who can be knocking at the door on such a cold night?"

He unbolted the door, and there rushed in, like a tempest, the unexpected apparition of the "big grandmother."

"Well!" she cried, "so I've come at last!"

"And you are welcome, mother," replied Max rising.

"You are welcome," said Doris. But she said to herself. "Goodness, where are we to put her to sleep? And what would she want for supper?"

Meanwhile the newcomer shook herself to rights, and made everybody help her get off her things.

"I have come to stay," she cried, "so you must get me up a bed somewhere. And do you, boys, see to my horse this instant."

The boys ran outside hurry-scurry, for next to each other they loved horses.

"Is there anything in this house to eat?" said the big grandmother. "Ah! Doris' mother, good evening."

"Thank you," said the little grandmother, and took up even less room in her chair than usual.

Minna brought out everything for supper she could think of, and Doris in a distracted way ran hither and thither, planning the beds. The maid, who had been sitting at her wheel fast asleep, now roused up, rubbed her eyes, and stumbled over the cat, whose pardon she begged, and tried to get awake enough to find out where she was.

The big grandmother sat at the table, and made havoc with everything, right and left. The younger children never took their eyes from her the whole while. At last she pushed back her chair, and burst forth with a long, hearty, boisterous laugh.

"Well?" she cried.

Nobody answered.

"Then you haven't heard the news?"

"We do not take a paper," said Max. "When there is anything new, I can read it at the tavern." "Pooh," she cried. "Well, I've taken another man!"

There was an awkward silence. Doris thought Max ought to say something, and Max hoped Doris would.

"Yes, another man. And I am going to live with him, instead of taking him to live with me. You shall see him presently."

And stepping to the door, with heavy tread, she blew a silver whistle that hung at her side.

In a few moments she ushered in her "man," and exhibited him with no little noisy laughter.

"He was made to order for me," she cried. "See! I am no infant, but he is head and shoulders above me. And now look in his face! Did you ever see a kinder or a handsomer one in all your lives?"

Indeed they never had. He was a man of colossal dimensions, and there beamed from his face a perfect flood of good humor and friendliness. His dress indicated that he was one of the rich overland farmers. He wore a black velvet coat adorned with immense silver buttons that almost touched each other, a scarlet vest, fastened in the same style, and the velvet band upon his wide hat was buckled with a silver buckle as long as his hand.

"Good evening," he said, smiling upon them like warm sunshine.

"Ha! ha! Now for the news, Max!" cried his mother. "Sit down, Conrad. You see, Max, my new man will not touch with his finger the house and lands left me by your father, neither will he look at the property I gained through Peter Fuchse. He is a rich man, and has more money than ten horses can draw. So what do you think he says to me? 'Divide your land and your goods among your children, and come with me, and live and die in peace.' Ha! ha! What do you say now, old fellow?"

Max had not a word to say, but sat bewildered in his chair, while Doris put her apron to her eyes, and the children sat openmouthed, unable to understand what was going on.

"So the house will be yours, Max," continued his mother, "and the farm and the barn, and everything, just as your father left them. The horses, and the cattle, and the hay, and the grain, I give you also, though heaven knows your blessed father never owned them. And all that came by Peter Fuchse shall go to your brother's wife and children, since I am his only heir, and he left no relations behind him. You can take your family to live in your father's house, and send the children to the Latin school all the rest of their days. Ha! ha! this is the best joke I ever heard of!"

"A joke indeed!" said Max.

"I hope it is one you all enjoy," said Conrad. "For your mother is not really in earnest in what she says. It is she who has the large kind heart, not I, as she would have you believe."

"Hold your tongue!" cried the grandmother. "Do not believe a word he says. I fought for my property three weeks and a day. Conrad would have me without, but not with it. He declared he would not enrich himself with money made by other men, and at last I had to yield. Ha! ha! And so good luck to you, Max Steiner, and may your old age be like mine!"

"There is not a word of truth in what she says," repeated Conrad. "The whole thing was planned and settled by her."

"There, go back to the tavern, and sleep, if you can, with so many falsehoods on your conscience. I declare it is almost midnight."

Little Lena awoke, and was astonished to see the lights and the strangers. She smiled at the silver buttons Conrad wore, which, compared with those of her father, were so many full moons. Conrad took the child in his gigantic arms, and she nestled close to his breast with instinctive friendliness.

"I am perfectly bewildered," said Max, "not knowing whether this is not, after all, a dream."

"It is a pleasant dream, nothing more," said Conrad. "But when you wake up from it, you will find yourself a rich man, as things go in this region."

He gave them each his hand and bade them good night. The children were now gotten off to bed, and the big grandmother was at last conducted to hers. She kept them awake the rest of the night by quarreling with the bed, which she said made it necessary to divide herself into two halves, and rest them by turns, and by bursting now and then into one of her boisterous "ha! ha's!"

But she was up in the morning at the rooster's crowing, as fresh and blooming as ever. She then gave each child a florin and a good slap on the shoulders, told them they might come to her wedding if they had anything fit to wear, and rode off with her Conrad with flying colors.

"Well! what do you think?" asked Max, when quiet was once more restored to the household.

"I don't know what to think," said Doris. "What do you say, dear mother?"

"I think our dear Lord means to have the boys educated," she answered.

"Then you don't think it is all a joke? And

whose plan is it? Conrad's, or my mother's?" asked Max.

"I think they planned it between them. Conrad may have put it into your mother's head, but I think she was quite willing to do as he wished. I always knew your mother had a good spot in her heart, and now that love has touched it—"

"Love!" cried Max. "Now, that is really too absurd!"

"She loves him, and is as happy as a child. And you may depend upon it, he will bring out all the good there is in her."

There was a long silence.

At last Max said:

"Then we shall all go back to live in my old home. And you will like that, mother."

It was the first time he had ever called her mother. She looked at him gratefully.

"Yes, Max, I shall like it. You cannot imagine how pleasant it will be to hear Pastor Koeffel preach."

"No, I cannot, for when I was a boy, I never pretended to listen to a word. Well, Doris, my little woman, what do you say?"

"I say, I don't care where my home is if you all are in it," she said. "But I dare say it will really seem like going home to live in our own dear old village once more. We shall have our old neighbors about us—and then, besides—you will let me give away just as much milk as I like, won't you, Max?"

Max replied by a merry laugh, and then the force of habit drove him to his workshop where he spent as busy a day as usual.

It was not so easy for Doris and the children to settle down to their work. The younger ones especially went to school with their heads, for the time, completely turned, while Herman rushed from one task to another in vain efforts to cool his fevered blood.

"To think that I can go back to the Latin school!" he said to himself. "And that Bernhard, who has so much sense, can go too! It seems like something out of a book, a fairy tale, or a fable, or else as if I had been asleep and had a beautiful dream!"

There was not a little commotion in the village, when the news of Max's good luck flew through it, growing as it flew. Babele Goschen sighed, and said it was hard that a poor lonely widow, who had never held up her head since the day of her husband's death, couldn't have had a little luck of the same sort.

"I fear their heads are all turned, poor things!" she cried. "Think now! The old mother is to have a little room quite to herself, out of the way of the noise of the house. And what with the quiet and the comfort, she'll live forever, or, at any rate, live till she dies of old age! As to Max, he was proud enough before, but now he'll be holding his head as high as the sky. And Doris will be worn out with care! Maids to see to, and nobody knows how much milk to look after and then that cross old mother of Max's flying back every now and then to find fault and bite all their heads off! And as for those boys, nothing will be good enough for them now! Well, well! I saw Herman sitting quite by himself yesterday, looking melancholy enough. I suppose it seems hard for him to have so many ups and downs and just as he had gotten to earning an honest penny, sent off to school once again!"

In the early spring Max and his household took flight to their new home, which they found awaiting them in perfect order, and where, with not much trouble, they settled down in peace and comfort. Even the little grandmother was thrown somewhat off her balance, when she saw the flocks and herds to which Max had become heir, saw his lambs and his cattle and his goods. To her and to Doris his new-found wealth seemed almost fabulous.

They began at once to form plans of usefulness in which they promised themselves to find the greatest joy. Life looked attractive, as their old neighbors began to flock about them. And then on Sundays there was the dear old Pastor Koeffel, silvery in hair and loving in face. And there was the Latin school waiting to welcome the boys. There was nothing that seemed lacking for their happiness.

Max had now reached the very highest aim of his ambition. He had more horses, more cattle, more land, than any of his neighbors. People looked up to him, and took counsel from him, and called him Herr Steiner. With his tendencies, so much sudden prosperity might have proved fatal to the Christian life which was beginning to soften and sanctify his rugged character. But he was no longer young, and the discipline through which he had passed had made a great impression. Then too, at the moment of temptation, he came under the influence of Pastor Koeffel, a man of rare piety, who never let his people forget that all they had belonged to God.

It is true that the habit of sparing and saving was not slain in a day. Max had always excused himself for his lack of generosity on the ground that he had so little to give. He found it, however, as hard to part with his money now that he was a comparatively rich man as it had been all his life long. It was only now and then, by a violent wrench upon his real nature, that he forced open his heart and gave of his abundance to the needy, while from Doris there flowed a constant stream of unnoticed charity which gladdened many a barren life.

As for her, like most women, she had but one ambition. To be a good wife and a good mother, and to be beloved by her husband and children, was all she asked. What she was in the old home, that she was in the new; a busy, affectionate, cheerful little housewife, whose voice would never be heard in the streets, but whose memory would always live in a few faithful hearts.

The children, however, entered upon their new life with enthusiasm. The boys rushed hither and thither; they made the acquaintance of every animal on the farm; they plowed a little and planted a little, and sowed a little; got in everybody's way; rode and drove to market, and frolicked in all the old haunts of their father's boyhood. When Max and Doris wanted to restrain them, their grandmother counseled that they should have full liberty, and the result proved her advice to be good, for after a few weeks they were all more than satisfied to settle down at school. Herman and Bernhard went together to the Latin school. Max had not decided to give them both equal advantages, but chose to see what the future would bring forth. Herman made up by perseverance and application for his natural lack of skill. It was a pleasure to see him engaged with his studies, when all the energies of his mind concentrated themselves on the work in hand. What he learned he never forgot, and every now and then a flash of real genius would reveal to his teachers what this modest, retiring boy really was. He never lost the desire and purpose to become a clergyman, and taking Pastor Koeffel for his model, he fought against the reserve and shyness which had thus far made his life so lonely, and mixed with the other boys, who learned to know and to love him.

As to Minna, she was in her element, now that she was full of housewifely cares. She took calm and serious satisfaction in overseeing the servants, in keeping the accounts, and generally in superintending her father's interests. The younger ones had their pet lambs and innumerable hens and chickens. They always managed to have on hand some lame or feeble animal, on which they found it expedient to lavish a wealth of love and tenderness and a depth of sympathy which, if bestowed on some desolate human heart, would have made it leap for sheer joy.

As time passed, and the elder boys proved, day by day, how worthy they were of the education they were receiving, people said their grandmother Steiner had been the making of them. And in her distant home she fondly thought and always said so herself. But she who gave only her prayers and the sweet influence of a holy life, whose name, so well known in heaven, was rarely spoken on earth, who never for a moment fancied she had anything to do with their training— she, perhaps, will one day hear from the Master's lips the "Well done, good and faithful servant!" which ushers into the joy of our Lord.

16

"Are you sure there is nothing left in the wagon? Let me see. There is the cheese, and here is the loaf of wheat bread. The roll of linen is all right. Yes, I believe everything is here. You can't say that I came empty-handed, Max!"

"We are glad to see you, mother, however you come," replied Max, whose arms were full of packages of all sorts. "But one would think we had a famine in the land to judge by the supplies you have brought with you."

"Pshaw! The linen is for Herman. As for those other things, they are for your Doris. A better wheat loaf she never ate. As for the cheese, the butter, and the sauerkraut, they will astonish her, and well they may. People at my time of life usually sit with folded hands, while I, thank heaven, expect to go on brewing and baking, mending and making, to the last breath I draw."

"I dare say you will. And so you have come to hear our Herman preach? It is very good of you, I'm sure."

"Nonsense! How can you suppose I made such a journey to hear that foolish boy? I am very angry with him for not choosing a profession that would bring distinction to the family. However, as he is really appointed to succeed Pastor Koeffel, and is going to live in the parsonage, I concluded to bring him a roll of linen, for I suppose your Doris has none to spare. Ah! Here she comes. How do you do, child? And how is your little mother? As strong and hearty as I am?"

"Mother is quite feeble," replied Doris. "She seldom leaves her room now. Will you step in to see her a moment?"

"I don't mind if I do. Well!" she shouted, as she entered the room, and saw the little grandmother reclining in an old-fashioned armchair.

"Yes, it is well," returned the other, looking up with a smile.

"There's nothing left of you but your eyes. And they are as bright as two beads. So, you just sit here, with nothing to do. Tedious enough, I dare say!"

"I just sit waiting," was the answer.

"Waiting? For whom, pray?"

Her days of embarrassment and confusion were over. She answered, with a simple dignity that almost overawed her gigantic questioner:

"For my *Master.*"

For once in her life, Max's mother felt embarrassed, and could think of nothing to say. She got out of the room as quickly as she could, and in a few moments her loud voice could be heard scolding her former maidens, Hedwig and Martha, who, poor things, wondered what they had done to deserve such treatment. Doris lingered behind.

"Dear mother," she said, kissing her, "don't talk so. We can't spare you, indeed we can't. Is there anything we can do to make you willing to stay with us?"

"You do everything, everything, dear child. But home looks very pleasant. And I shall go soon." Doris wiped her eyes more than once, as she moved about the house, attending to the household cares involved in the unexpected visit of Max's mother, with her Conrad.

"Ah! how much richer is my mother, who has not a florin in the world, than they are!" she thought. "I wish heaven seemed as near to me as it does to her! But, oh! I feel bound, as with chains, to Max, to the children and to this pleasant home!"

There was no little bustle and confusion in the house at this time. Herman had passed through his preparatory course, and was to take the place of Pastor Koeffel, who now slept in the church-yard among his people, like a father with his children around him. Bernhard had come home to spend the first Sunday of the new pastorate, prepared to admire his brother's preaching as much as he had done in the days of their boyhood. Max's mother had come on the same errand, say what she might to the contrary. Max and Doris hardly knew whether they felt most pride and pleasure, or most nervous anxiety, at the thought of seeing the fresh and youthful face of their Herman in the pulpit, where for so many years Pastor Koeffel had instructed them.

"Dear mother," said Doris, lingering behind the rest, as they set forth for church, "you have looked forward to this day so long, and now you cannot hear Herman after all. Are you very much disappointed?" She never forgot the sweetness and the brightness of the smile which accompanied the reply:

"No, dear child. I have traveled beyond disappointments."

As she walked on by Max's side, she revolved these words in her mind, wondering what they signified. "Mother doesn't mean that she's gotten beyond caring for things, for she never was so interested in all that concerns us. She grows more loving every day. I don't quite see what she does mean. I haven't traveled beyond disappointments, at any rate, for if Herman should make a blunder, and leave out part of the service, or anything of that sort, I know I would never get over it. How my heart beats! To think now that my Herman, who everybody used to call such a dunce, should really be Herr Pastor after all!"

"I suppose they'll be holding their heads higher than ever, now that their Herman has actually come to be Herr Pastor," said Babele Goschen, as she adjusted her Sunday cap above her withered features. "I've two minds not to go to hear him preach after all. It's somebody's duty to put him down and keep him down, I say."

"I dare say he wouldn't miss us if we did stay away," returned Lizette. "And I mean to go. It's nothing but envy that makes you talk so."

"I won't have my own children throwing my faults in my face," cried Babele. "It's enough to make a saint envious to see how things have gone on with that boy, and all of them. And it is hard, and I don't care who hears me say it, to do as well by children as I've done by mine, and then have them turn out as they have. Kurt getting ready to lie down in a tippler's grave, like his father before him, and you so sassy and self-willed that there's no peace with you."

"I hope you'll hear something in the sermon that will be blessed to you," returned Lizette. "If you had gone to church, and brought us up as you ought, we might have turned out more to your mind. I'm sure I wish you had. But come, it is time to go. It's an hour and a half to the village, if it's a minute. And you get out of breath if one hurries in the least."

Babele made no answer, and the two set forth together for a long walk which led to the church of Pastor Koeffel.

When they entered the church, the service had not yet begun, and Babele had time to look about her, and to make remarks at her leisure.

"Here comes Max and Doris! Look, Lizette! Doris looks all in a flutter. There, she dropped her prayer book, and there goes her handkerchief. Now Minna is picking them up. I might wait till I was gray before you'd do as much for me."

"Please stop talking mother," said Lizette. "Everybody is so still and solemn. Besides, I want to catch the first glimpse of Herman when he comes into church. He'll come in with an air, you may depend."

"There's Max's mother, I declare!" cried Babele, in such a loud whisper that Max heard the well-known voice. He glanced at his old neighbor kindly, and the color rose in his face to his forehead.

"Our dear Lord has been too good to me!" he said to himself, "since the days when Babele used to make us her visits. And she looks so worn out and so anxious. We'll have her home to dinner with us, poor creature."

"He needn't turn so red at the sight of me," was Babele's secret thought. "I am not going to speak to him or his, unless they speak to me. And if they are ashamed of their old neighbor, why, let them be ashamed, that's all."

At this moment there was a little stir in the church, and the young Pastor came in. He had developed into a full-grown man of his father's height, but the slight resemblance he had borne him in his childhood had quite disappeared. Otherwise, to the casual observer, he looked like an ordinary, good sort of young man, such as one sees by the score every day.

"He isn't handsome, that's one comfort," thought Babele. "And he hasn't got much of a voice, that's another thing." Her mind wandered away during the preliminary services. She counted the buttons on Max's vest, estimated the cost of Minna's red petticoat, of which she could see a fragment, felt a little sleepy, and was suddenly aroused by the announcement of the text:

For I determined not to know anything among you, save Jesus Christ, and Him crucified. And I was with you in weakness, and in fear, and in much trembling.

"You never spoke a truer word," said Babele,

nodding at the young speaker, as if he could hear what she said. "I suppose you're going to preach about yourself, and tell what a smart man folks say you are, and what fools we all were not to find you out sooner. Brag away! It's just what I've come to hear."

She settled herself comfortably in her seat, gave a glance at Lizette, and the sermon began. Curiosity kept her awake, tired as she was with her long walk from her own village, and, in spite of herself, the growing eloquence and earnestness of the speaker soon made her forget where she was, or to whom she listened. When at last she thought to look around her, to see the effect of the sermon, she was almost appalled by the solemnity of every face. Even her giddy Lizette sat motionless, her hands in her lap, her eyes fixed upon the glowing face now transfigured into something more beautiful than beauty, while tear after tear rolled down her unconscious cheek. Doris sat leaning forward a little, the timid delight with which she listened at first had given way to absorbing interest in the subject.

"He ain't preaching about himself, after all," thought Babele. "To hear him go on, one would think the Lord Jesus was his best friend, and that he'd rather praise Him than magnify himself. How his color comes and goes! It seems as if everything he said came out of a deep well, and he wore himself out hauling it up."

"Humph! Just *like him!*"

This irreverent exclamation proceeded from the big grandmother, and was heard all over the church, for at this point a sweep of Herman's sleeve brushed his sermon from the pulpit desk, and the loose leaves went flying about the church like so many frightened birds.

Max reddened with shame and vexation. Doris rose from her seat, and sank back again in despair. For an instant the youthful speaker faltered and became pale, but before the startled congregation had time to recover from its surprise, or the nimblest foot to hasten to the rescue, he went bravely, eloquently on. No longer fettered by written words, he poured forth a flood of eloquence which made every man, woman and child completely forget the interruption, or even to rejoice in it.

"Well, Lizette, how did you like him?" asked Babele, when the sermon at last came to an end.

"Do be still, mother," was the reply, in an angry whisper.

"You cried, at any rate," persisted Babele.

"It's no such thing!"

Max and Doris longed to talk over their new experience together in private, but they both came kindly to Babele, to invite her to dine with them.

"I suppose you are as proud as peacocks, now," she said. "And to be sure, your Herman looks very well in gown and bands. They quite set him off. But isn't his preaching rather odd, and out of the common way? Why, I understood every word of it!"

Doris, too humble to have an opinion of her own on the subject, looked anxious and concerned. But before she had time to answer, Max's mother, who had come striding after them, burst out with:

"You're a fool, Babele Goschen! Of course, his preaching is out of the common way. He's got sense enough to say things out of his own head, and that nobody ever thought of before. Ha! that's just the difference between Herman and me, and all the rest of you. We've got something to say, and we say it with a vengeance. If he had preached in the humdrum way most young fellows do, I'd have pulled him down from the pulpit, and pitched him into the Neckar River."

Babele subsided in the presence of this woman, who dared to speak of ministers as "fellows," and who talked of plunging the successor of the revered Pastor Koeffel into the Neckar.

"I meant no offense," she said. "And I hope you'll take none."

"I hate apologies. But I can tell you one thing: you never in your entire life heard such a sermon as you heard today. Even I, who never shed tears, cried like rain. And I declare I didn't know it was such a delicious thing to cry. Why, it's next best to laughing."

17

Meanwhile, Doris' mother lay back peacefully in her chair, the Bible from which she had been reading, open on a little table by her side. She read nothing now save the gospel narrative concerning her Savior, her increasing love to Him giving to every word that fell from His lips when He lived on earth a rare preciousness such as she had only known of late.

Hedwig, whose duty it was to watch over her in the absence of the household, looked in every half hour to see that she lacked nothing, otherwise she was left quite alone, as was her wish. In this sweet Sabbath stillness she prayed silently for each member of the family, but especially for her beloved Herman, that he might make full proof of his ministry, and that the word he preached this day might prove as good seed, sown in good soil, for the glory of Jesus Christ. Then she prayed for Max, for Doris, for Minna, Bernhard, and Adolph, each by name, and with a strange earnestness that made her quite unconscious of the feeble body that held her glowing soul. Then she prayed for Max's mother and her Conrad, that they might see the King in His beauty, as she herself now saw Him. And it is not saying too much of these simple prayers that were almost wordless, that they were heard and answered while she was yet speaking. We cannot remind ourselves too often that no prayer is poverty-stricken that is offered in His name who presents our petitions for us to the Father.

Herman, under the influence of these apparently feeble words, was at that moment speaking as one inspired, and finding his way to every heart in the congregation. Even his big grandmother, though she would not admit it to herself, felt herself touched to the core. She could not help being convinced that the things of which he spoke were real, that he had held converse with the Christ whom he preached and that he valued his own natural gifts chiefly as something to lay at His feet.

As they all sat together at dinner, she gave him no peace.

"To think, now, of you flinging your sermon at the very heads of the people!" she cried. "You are just as clumsy as when you were a boy." Herman blushed painfully. He was ashamed of himself that he could not bear her scoffing without wincing under it, but his whole heart had been thrown into his sermon, and he had come down from the heights to which he had soared, to find himself a very common mortal, as vulnerable as ever, if possible even more so.

Max, seeing his distress, came to the rescue.

"No harm was done!" he cried. "It was a fine thing to see the boy go on preaching as well without his sermon as with it. And the last half was the best, after all."

"His gestures are positively frightful," pursued the merciless foe. "If I hadn't been crying, I would have laughed at the way he flung his arms about and at the grimaces he made. Once or twice I thought he was going to beat out his brains."

"One is often tempted to wish it no sin to do that," replied Herman, who was now quite down from the mount, and felt exceedingly flat.

"Your grandmother has an odd way of expressing her approbation," said Conrad, "but you must know her well enough by this time not to mind what she says."

"I'm sure he will improve as he grows older,"

said Babele Goschen in a patronizing tone, which somehow was more excruciating to Herman than his grandmother's random shots.

"Come, mother, it's time to go," said Lizette, who had sense enough to see that these words were not making a very favorable impression.

And as they drove home in Max's wagon, she added, crossly enough:

"I wish you knew when to hold your tongue, mother. The idea of Herman's improving, when he is as good as an angel now! I don't believe you even listened to the sermon. If you had, you never could have eaten such an enormous dinner."

"What was the dinner for, if not to eat?" was the reply. "And with such poor pickings as I get at home, a decent dinner is more to my mind than your fine preaching, not that I've any fault to find with that either."

Relieved by the departure of her guests, Doris flew to her mother to pour out her morning's experiences into her loving ear. But suddenly she paused in the flow of her talk.

"Do you feel worse than usual, dear mother?" she asked.

"No, dear, better than usual. I feel well in body and well in soul. This has been a blessed day, my Doris."

Doris looked at the radiant yet very colorless face.

"I think I must stay and be your nurse this afternoon," she said. "I can hear Herman instruct the children some other time, just as well."

"Yes and you will have the evening service to attend," said her mother.

This tacit consent to her remaining at home alarmed Doris even more than her mother's unusual paleness had done. But she talked on cheerfully, putting away the unwelcome, vague fears that oppressed her, to be met at some more convenient moment.

"I want to be happy today, of all days, she thought. And she did have a very happy afternoon. Her mother seemed so like herself, and said so many things she afterward recalled with pleasure. She repeated many little sayings and doings of the children in their younger days that Doris had long since forgotten, and now heard with curious interest. And then she went back over all the way in which the Lord had led her, speaking of her Master with a tender, personal affection, which made the heart of Doris glow, while she said to herself, "Oh! that I loved Him so!"

At eventide the rest of the family returned from church, and after supper they all gathered in their grandmother's room to sing hymns. Max's mother, with her Conrad, held aloof, yet, as the sounds of their cheerful voices reached her in her room, she felt herself once more moved even to tears.

"Bah!" she cried to Conrad, who looked at her with surprise. "I am not crying. My eyes have been weak all day."

When the singing was over, each one gave their grandmother the goodnight kiss before leaving her. Doris lingered a little behind, with some expressions of endearment, and then followed the rest to supper.

"Let me take her supper to grandmother tonight," said Herman. "It is my last chance."

"Oh! no," said Doris quickly, not understanding that he referred to his own removal to the parsonage. "Mother has not seemed so bright and like herself in a long time."

Herman made no answer. He had observed and been alarmed by his grandmother's unusual appearance, for he was already becoming experienced in sick rooms. He was hardly gone an instant, when he returned. One glance at his face made everybody spring from the table.

Ah, how near heaven is! How little time it takes to get there! In one brief moment she who had so long sat waiting for her Lord had heard His voice, and had gone joyfully to meet Him. The smile with which she had welcomed Him still lingered on and illuminated her face.

Doris ran and clasped the small, worn figure in her arms.

"Oh, mother! mother! speak to me once more, only once more!" she cried.

Max rushed out for the doctor. He knew it was too late, but he could not bear the sight of such distress.

"Oh! what an ending to this happy Sunday!" sobbed Doris. "Where is Herman?"

She instinctively turned to him for sympathy, who was now her pastor as well as her son.

"It is a beautiful ending, dear mother!" said Herman. "This is not death, it is a translation!" His lips quivered, however, for he had loved his grandmother with a peculiar affection, and after a momentary struggle with himself, he burst into tears. God knows the opportune moment at which to send sorrow into a house, and it is His goodness and mercy that does not suffer the cup of earthly happiness to become too full. It was with a tempered joy and under the holy shadow of a real sorrow that he entered on the work of the ministry, and settled down among the people to whom Pastor Koeffel had so long ministered. Minna went with him to the parsonage to arrange his household, and helped him to make it a refuge for the weary, and the resort of all who suffered in body or mind.

Max and Doris devoted themselves less and less to making money, and more and more to spending it on those who lacked. They lived many long, useful, happy years in the home of his childhood, and their children and children's children rose up to call them blessed. Bernhard completed his studies at the university, where in time, he was chosen to be a professor. His grandmother Steiner took the whole credit for this event to herself, and, as no one disputed it with her, it continued to be to her a lifelong source of glorification. Though she never tamed into a model woman, the progress of years and the discipline of life softened her somewhat, and before her death she said and did some things that enabled Max to say of her, after she was gone:

"My mother had her peculiarities. I never saw anybody exactly like her, but I believe she died a saved woman at last."

As for Adolph and Lena, amidst the waywardness of their youth they still wore some fragments of her mantle whose saintly memory lingered long in her native village. As time passed, they too learned to reverence and to profit by the ministry of the "Little Preacher," whose self-distrust had only given way to an invincible modesty that made both young and old love to sit at his feet and learn of Jesus.

STATEMENT OF FAITH

We believe in One God existing in three persons – Father, Son and Holy Spirit (Jer 10:10, Deut 6:4, Isa 44:6, Matt 28:18-20, John 14:16, II Cor 13:14).

We believe that Jesus Christ is both true God and true man (John 1:1-4, Gal 4:4). That Jesus died on the cross for the sins of mankind (Heb 9:22-28, I Pet 2:24, 3:18, Romans 5:6-8, Gal 1:4). That he was bodily resurrected the third day (I Cor 15:3-7, Luke 24:1-8). We believe that Jesus Christ ascended into heaven (Luke 24:50, Acts 1:9-11), and that he is coming again (John 14:3, Acts 1:11, I Cor 15:51-52).

We believe that the Bible is God's holy word, disclosing the way to salvation (Rom 1:16). We believe the Word of God to be God breathed, and thus by this standard we live our lives (2 Tim 3:16-17, I Cor 15:1-2).

HSM MISSION STATEMENT

We here at HSM desire to encourage our brothers and sisters in Christ by providing only the finest in Christian Literature. Books that not only entertain, but uphold the truths of scripture and delight the soul. We hold to the truth in Romans 12:2 "And to not be conformed to this world, but be transformed by the renewing of your mind, so that you may prove what the will of God is, that which is good and acceptable and perfect".